"As I was reading, I began compiling a list of people I'd like to get a copy of *Ruthless* to. But the more I read, the more I realized how desperately *I* needed to read the life-transforming words in this book. Bo sheds new light on ancient words, compelling us to dive deeply to discover the character of the One who fights for each of us."

—SHELLY JOHNSON, director of women's ministries,
New Heights Church, Vancouver, Washington

"In today's pluralistic culture with so many opinions about God, Bo has written not as a theorist but as a practitioner of the truth of the God she has come to know personally. You can't read this without your assumptions being tested as you come face to face with the God of Bo and the Bible—a good and ruthless God who is love."

—REV. TAMMY DUNAHOO, general supervisor,
The Foursquare Church

"Bo Stern has a distinct way of drawing us closer to the heart of God. In *Ruthless*, she gives not only good ideas and comforting words but also a message of enduring hope and steadfast confidence in our God, who can be deeply known and completely trusted in our deepest areas of need."

—DEBI MILLS, women's and marriage pastor

*Jenny,*
*May His presence*
*be your great*
*reward.*
*Bo Stern*

# RUTHLESS

## KNOWING THE GOD
## WHO FIGHTS FOR YOU

# BO STERN

NAVPRESS
Discipleship Inside Out®

**NAVPRESS**
Discipleship Inside Out®

NavPress is the publishing ministry of The Navigators, an international Christian organization and leader in personal spiritual development. NavPress is committed to helping people grow spiritually and enjoy lives of meaning and hope through personal and group resources that are biblically rooted, culturally relevant, and highly practical.

**For a free catalog go to www.NavPress.com**
**or call 1.800.366.7788 in the United States or 1.800.839.4769 in Canada.**

NAVPRESS and the NAVPRESS logo are registered trademarks of NavPress. Absence of ® in connection with marks of NavPress or other parties does not indicate an absence of registration of those marks.

ISBN-13: 978-1-61291-602-6

Some of the anecdotal illustrations in this book are true to life and are included with the permission of the persons involved. All other illustrations are composites of real situations, and any resemblance to people living or dead is coincidental.

Unless otherwise identified, all Scripture quotations in this publication are taken from the Holman Christian Standard Bible® (HCSB), copyright © 1999, 2000, 2002, 2003, 2009 Holman Bible Publishers, used by permission. Holman Christian Standard Bible®, Holman CSB®, and HCSB® are federally registered trademarks of Holman Bible Publishers. Other versions used include: the *Holy Bible, New International Version*® (NIV®). Copyright © 1973, 1978, 1984, 2011 by Biblica, Inc.® Used by permission of Zondervan. All rights reserved worldwide. www.zondervan.com. The "NIV" and "New International Version" are trademarks registered in the United States Patent and Trademark Office by Biblica, Inc.® ; the *Amplified Bible* (AMP), © 1954, 1958, 1962, 1964, 1965, 1987 by The Lockman Foundation, used by permission; *THE MESSAGE* (MSG), copyright © 1993, 1994, 1995, 1996, 2000, 2001, 2002, used by permission of NavPress Publishing Group; New English Translation (NET) NET Bible® copyright ©1996–2006 by Biblical Studies Press, L.L.C. All rights reserved; and the King James Version (KJV).

Stern, Bo.
  Ruthless : knowing the God who fights for you / Bo Stern.
      pages cm
  Includes bibliographical references.
  ISBN 978-1-61291-602-6
  1. God (Christianity)  I. Title.
  BT103.S735 2014
  231--dc23
                                2013039332

Printed in the United States of America
1 2 3 4 5 6 7 8 / 19 18 17 16 15 14

*For my parents, Stan and Ellen Mishler, whose lives have given me a window into the character of God and the faith to believe He is always and only beautiful.*

# CONTENTS

# ACKNOWLEDGMENTS

I love to write, and sometimes I'm a mess when I write. Frustrated. Frustrating. Anxious. Focused. Scattered. Scared. The fact that my family and friends are still with me when I reach The End is evidence of their bravery and beauty. I am so thankful for these stout hearts who are generous with their encouragement and unconditional with their love.

Whitney Parnell, daughter and assistant extraordinaire—I am beyond thankful for your hard work, wisdom, and friendship. Corey and Greyson Parnell—Thank you for sharing Whitney and for adding so much life, love, and Irish to Team Stern.

Victoria Stern—You share my love of words and my dream of a world free of unnecessary quotation marks. Your future is filled with hope, sweet girl. Don't you doubt it for a minute.

Tess Stern—You are strong and courageous and my favorite person to shop with. Thank you for knowing Him and showing His goodness to a watching world.

Josiah Stern—How did you get so tall? And strong? And wonderful? I'm a million ways thankful that you are mine.

Our family, friends, and co-laborers at Westside Church—Oh, how I love you!

Mekenzie Stearns, friend and research assistant—Thank you for working with my scatterbrained system and demonstrating patience above and beyond the call of duty and the limits of Dropbox. I'm so blessed by you.

To all who have experienced the devastation of ALS: You are my country. I will stand with you until a cure is common and the disease is rare.

Steve Stern—You are the proof that not all superheroes wear capes. I adore you. Forever.

With deep love, I remember and honor the life of Paul Stern. Not only did he give me his youngest son, but his investment in the kingdom of God has influenced my life in profound ways.

I don't have the words to acknowledge the work of God in my life, which I deeply hope is reflected in these pages. He is everything. Everything. All I can do is borrow the prayer of Jesus: Father, glorify Your name.

# INTRODUCTION

*Let not the wise boast of their wisdom or the strong boast of their strength
or the rich boast of their riches, but let the one who boasts boast about this:
that they have the understanding to know me, that I am the LORD, who
exercises kindness, justice and righteousness on earth, for in these I delight.*

JEREMIAH 9:23-24 (NIV)

Imagine that you came to me to say that a man had driven by
you in his car, rolled down his window, hurled a rock at you,
and called you ugly. How do you think I would respond? I can
assure you that I would be furious. I would be so angry, in fact,
that I would want to go get that guy and teach him a lesson in
manners. I would be spitting mad at this injustice and ready to
defend your cause at (nearly) any price.

Now imagine you told me that my husband, Steve, had
driven by you, thrown a rock at you, and called you ugly.
Entirely different situation. How would I respond? I would tell
you without hesitation, "You've got the wrong guy." I *know*

Steve Stern. I've been married to him for twenty-eight years. That's twenty-eight years of conversations and family vacations and bounced checks and hard nights and fierce fights. I know him, and I've never known a more compassionate man. I've seen him rock our sick children through the night and tenderly care for their bike-crashing wounds. I was with him in a restaurant once when an older man who was recovering from surgery fell over and began bleeding from his head. While everyone else scattered, Steve got down on the floor, put the man's head in his lap, and started praying and speaking soft words over him. I *know* Steve. I know his character.

Even if you could produce a DNA sample from the rock itself, I would still tell you, "You got the wrong guy. My husband does not throw rocks at people."

In my first book, *Beautiful Battlefields*, I told the story of Steve's diagnosis of Amyotrophic Lateral Sclerosis (ALS) and how God has used this fight to make both of us stronger in our faith and purpose than we have ever been. Since then, I've been inundated with stories from readers who are also facing a fierce Goliath. Often the summation of their battle is this desperate question: "Why would God do this to me?"

Oh, friend, I sympathize with the question, I really do. I know it's hard to understand the purpose in pain and suffering, but I will tell you with certainty: You've got the wrong guy.

God doesn't throw rocks at us.

He is good and does good (see Psalm 119:68), and He lives to love us into abundant life (see John 10:10). That's who He is, and you need to understand this truth if you're going to trust

Him with your triumphs and tragedies. Having nearly twenty years in ministry has taught me that most of the struggles people face in their faith are the result of a misinformed or undeveloped view of God. Many people pledge their lives to a God they don't yet know (which is fine) but then don't take the time to get to know Him (which isn't).

*Theology* is a big, boring-sounding word, but it means nothing more than the study of God—who He is and what He does. We can survive theological gaps and misunderstandings when things are going well in our lives, but when we're faced with a Really Big Battle, it's essential that we determine what we believe to be true of our Battle Commander and then stick to that truth like glue. We need to know The God Who Fights For Us or we will be tempted to turn to ourselves or other sources for help, and that's always a bad idea that often leads to a bigger battle.

Now, some people believe we can't really know God. They say He's too big and grand and mysterious and that to presume we can know Him is the height of arrogance. But this belief causes us to live with an underlying fear of His power and punishment or to distance ourselves from Him, treating Him like an ancient creed to which we have ascribed devotion but in whom we find no delight. Or it causes us to cross our fingers and hope He's not mad at us because we aren't sure what He's capable of and we're just trying to stay on His sunny side. It can seem daunting if not downright impossible to really know God.

I agree that God cannot be dissected and put under the microscope like a science project. We will never unravel the beautiful mystery that makes up the omni-everything of His nature. But I contend that we can know many things about Him, and we can know them with the kind of certainty that gives us strength, peace, and—dare I say—joy in the middle of our fiercest fights. This is not theory to me. I believe it because I'm living it out on my own brutal battleground right now. My theology over the course of this fight with ALS has grown increasingly simple but increasingly strong. The things I know, I know for sure, and this assurance is a powerful weapon in my arsenal (perhaps even the *most* powerful weapon I possess). I am fastened to the truth of God's character, and no force from any realm can shake me from it. Knowing I am loved by a God who is actively involved in my battle and deals ruthlessly with my enemies grows more important to me every day.

In order to build a résumé, so to speak, for God's character, we are going to turn to His Word over and over again. Prepare to wear out the hinges of your Bible as we travel into its pages, building a list of words that describe who God is and what He does. We will focus entirely on *Him*. This will be an interesting endeavor because God's Word is deep water and it's not always as clear as we would like it to be. The Bible doesn't offer much in the way of well-organized lists or PowerPoint slides to outline and demonstrate the attributes of the Sovereign God. Instead, this ancient-but-still-alive book throws open its doors and invites us into the beautiful mess of battles and weddings, feasts and famine, heartache and hope, showing us case studies of the character of the God who resides over the expanse of human history.

At the end of each day's reading, you will have a chance to

dream a little and wrestle these truths of His nature into your own belief system. I will nudge your imagination with questions that are not meant to stump you but rather to inspire you to establish an immovable relationship with the One who loves you without condition and without end. As you see God at work in the history of the world, you'll begin to see Him at work in the here and now of your fights and fears, standing strong and relentless against the enemies you face. My deepest prayer is that as you read these pages, you will feel this truth sink into your bones: He is The God Who Fights For You. Ruthlessly. As that truth takes root, so will the awareness that you are not alone and, therefore, you don't have to be as strong, smart, or scrappy as you once believed. He is more than enough for the win.

## WORTH PONDERING

1. Before we launch into chapter 1, take a moment to list a few things you know to be true about God.

2. Now list some areas where you have questions about who He is and how or why He works the way He does (Is He really trustworthy? Does He really love me?).

*The God Who Fights For You . . .*

# STANDS BIGGER THAN YOUR BATTLE

In 2011, when my husband was diagnosed with ALS, we knew we were in for the fight of our lives. ALS is always fatal and carries a prognosis of two to five years, during which time it slowly paralyzes its victims until only their eyes and brain function. When we got the news, I felt overwhelmed and surrounded by giants on every side. I remember in the first few weeks thinking there was no way to win because this enemy was so much bigger than our abilities or intelligence. But then I stumbled onto Sennacherib.

The story of Sennacherib's attack on Judah is told in Isaiah 36 and 37 (and also 2 Kings 19 and 2 Chronicles 32). Sennacherib was king of Assyria, a vicious and powerful nation that had stormed through Judah's smaller cities and now was knocking on Jerusalem's door. Nearly 200,000 soldiers surrounded Judah's capital city, shouting threats over the wall, and then

King Sennacherib formalized those threats by sending a letter to King Hezekiah of Judah, outlining all the ways he planned to destroy Jerusalem. Sennacherib wasn't bluffing; his army had the power, passion, and experience necessary to do exactly as he promised. The city of Jerusalem was doomed and desperate.

I can imagine how Hezekiah felt, reading those words from the evil king. I remember holding our doctor's official diagnosis in my hands, trying to breathe through the tears and hoping to wake up and discover it was all a terrible dream. I felt suffocated by the size of the enemy and surrounded by the pressing decisions that come along with a Really Big Battle. I'm guessing you've felt it too. I bet you've held a similar "letter" of your own. At some point in life, it seems all of us will face an enemy well outside our weight class. In those moments, we feel small, inadequate and alone, and I'm guessing that even though Hezekiah wore the title *King*, he felt that way too. We can learn so much from the way Hezekiah responded:

> Hezekiah received the letter from the messengers and read it. Then he went up to the temple of the Lord and spread it out before the Lord. And Hezekiah prayed to the Lord: "Lord Almighty, the God of Israel, enthroned between the cherubim, you alone are God over all the kingdoms of the earth. You have made heaven and earth. Give ear, Lord, and hear; open your eyes, Lord, and see; listen to all the words Sennacherib has sent to ridicule the living God." (Isaiah 37:14-17, NIV)

Hezekiah could have rallied his army, gathered his weapons, or run for the hills. Instead, he turned to the only One he knew was bigger than Sennacherib. Take a look at how the story turns as he prays. Hezekiah positioned God at the head of the fight and then, in a truly brilliant battle maneuver, took himself out of the skirmish altogether. Read the last line again:

> Give ear, LORD, and hear; open your eyes, LORD, and see; listen to all the words Sennacherib has sent to *ridicule the living God.*
> (emphasis added)

Hezekiah clearly understood that he and his city stood in the shadow of the supremely powerful God. When the Assyrians picked a fight with Judah, they picked a fight with Judah's God. And Judah's God was in no mood for this nonsense:

> This is what the LORD, the God of Israel, says: "Because you have prayed to me concerning Sennacherib king of Assyria, this is the word the LORD has spoken against him. . . .
>
> "I will defend this city and save it,
>     for my sake and for the sake of David my servant!"
>
> Then the angel of the LORD went out and put to death a hundred and eighty-five thousand in the Assyrian camp. When the people got up the next morning — there were all the dead bodies! (verses 21-22,35-36, NIV)

When Hezekiah turned to God for help and trusted Him to ride first into the battle, He dealt ruthlessly with Hezekiah's enemies. I've found this true in my life as well. When I let God fight for me, He always wins. I don't have Philistines or Assyrians lined up in my driveway, so I have to remind myself who my enemy really is. On paper, it might look like our battle is with ALS, but actually our fight is against the things that have the power to damage our souls and destroy our purpose, such as hopelessness, bitterness, and unbelief. As Steve and I position God at the head of our battle, He fights for us and we experience the real win: a fresh infusion of hope and a clear focus on eternity, where all the books will be balanced and all bodies mended. I'm convinced that learning to trust Him with modern-day monsters such as financial crises, relationship breakdowns, and deadly diagnoses is one of most important battle skills we can build.

No matter what your fight today, our big God is one prayer away. He heard and responded to Hezekiah; He will hear and defend you from the Evil One's attempts to steal, kill, and destroy. As we launch into this study of God's character, let's start with the understanding that He is bigger than any bully we'll ever face. When our enemy comes calling, our great God can be trusted to answer the door.

More reading: Exodus 15:2-3; Deuteronomy 20:1; Isaiah 9:7; 42:13; 59:17

## WORTH PONDERING

1. Write down the names of the biggest giants you're facing.

2. Now write down the ways you know that God is bigger than those giants.

## CHAPTER 2

*The God Who Fights For You . . .*

# DOES GOOD ALWAYS

*God is good.* Everything else we believe about Him is supported or subverted by our understanding of this unchanging truth. It's the one thing to know when the chips are down. When you find yourself in a Really Big Battle, the rock-solid certainty that God is *always* good will be your best weapon in the fight.

Yes, He is all-knowing, omnipresent, entirely strong, and eternally unchanging, but these superpowers are not good news if they rest in the hands of a temperamental, spiteful, or unkind God. "Absolute power corrupts absolutely," goes the saying, and history has proven it true. But when absolute power rests in the hands of a God who is always and only good, we small humans can trust that He will use His power to restore and redeem our world.

Here is one of my favorite statements about the goodness of God, made by none other than God Himself (through the prophet Jeremiah):

> I will make an everlasting covenant with them: I will never turn
> away from doing good to them, and I will put fear of Me in their
> hearts so they will never again turn away from Me. I will take
> delight in them to do what is good for them, and with all My
> heart and mind I will faithfully plant them in this land.
> (32:40-41)

Would you go back and read that verse out loud and let the truth of it sink into your heart? (By the way, I'll ask you to do this many times throughout the chapters that follow because I believe strongly in the power of speaking out the Word of God, so plan to read this book in a place where you can speak out loud freely.)

You might offer a protest at this point. "But this was God's promise to the Israelites more than 2,700 years ago!" Yes. So true. I agree that it is unwise to pluck a verse out of the middle of a text without understanding the who, when, and why of what was really being said and then try to paste it over our own situation. However, that's not what we're doing here. In this book, we are working to understand God's character, not His promises *to us*. We are building a résumé for God's ability (what He does) and integrity (how He does it) so we can know whether He is worth trusting with our lives and futures. So for our purposes, whether this promise applies to us is not the point. The point is that God makes some wildly extravagant claims about His goodness.

The Israelites, the people to whom God was speaking, had abandoned their allegiance to Him time and time again. They were now being chased down by the Babylonians and were about to be carried into decades of captivity. They had been unfaithful in every way. They had rejected His covenant and His correction and chosen to serve other gods instead, and now their own king had thrown Jeremiah in prison. It's into this sorry situation that God spoke. Read the promise one more time:

> I will make an everlasting covenant with them: I will never turn away from doing good to them . . . . I will take delight in them to do what is good for them, and with all My heart and mind I will faithfully plant them in this land.

Can you believe it? Can you believe that God would trust the Israelites again? Can you imagine a God with the power to wipe them off the face of the earth and start over, choosing instead to chase them down with His goodness? Every time I read this, my heart leaps with the wonder of it all. God gives two, three, and three million chances to those He loves. He is good and His goodness is not static or passive. It pursues us and plants us. It seeks and saves us.

The word *everlasting* suggests to me that who God has been to sinful, unfaithful Israel He will also be to sinful, unfaithful Bo. People change; God does not. His character then is His character now, so I can trust that He. Is. Good. Always and in all ways. God is good, and that truth alone is strong enough to support the weight of my life and my battle.

A friend of mine who does not share my faith recently

asked me, "How can you believe that God is good when He has allowed your husband to have ALS?" It's an excellent question. I've read a lot of highly educated, extremely complicated ideas on this topic, but the answer seems very simple to me: The goodness of God does not keep us from all evil. Jesus said, "In this world you will have trouble. But take heart! I have overcome the world" (John 16:33, NIV). We don't have to look far or hard to find trouble. Our world is swarming with it because we have a very big enemy in Satan. Trouble comes from his attempts to destroy us and from our own sin and mistakes. Salvation does not inoculate us from experiencing the evil that runs rampant throughout humanity's bloodstream; rather, it keeps our hearts held safely in God's goodness, even in the midst of the hard times that are inevitable in our fallen world. His love follows us onto every battlefield and turns it into a place where beauty grows. I hate ALS and so does God. When the day is hard or the battle is hot, I remember this one thing: He will not be in debt to me. He is fighting for us, and His goodness will have the last word.

More reading: Psalm 25:8; 34:8; 86:5; 100:5; 103:5; 135:3; 145:9; Nahum 1:7; 1 Peter 2:3

## WORTH PONDERING

1. What are some ways you have seen the goodness of God in general? In your life specifically?

2. What keeps you from believing that God is always good (as opposed to sometimes good)?

## CHAPTER 3

*The God Who Fights For You . . .*
# ISN'T MAD AT YOU

We live in a dog-eat-dog world. For those optimistic souls who believe that humankind is predominantly good at heart, a few minutes watching the nightly news will pop that bubble fast. Around every corner, someone is being sued, slandered, or maligned. Mercy and grace are a steadily shrinking commodity in this survival-of-the-fittest society. That's what makes the compassion of God so beautiful and strong. It's an attribute of His nature I depend on every day. Look at these examples from His Word:

> The LORD is compassionate and gracious,
> slow to anger and rich in faithful love.
> He will not always accuse us
> or be angry forever.
> He has not dealt with us as our sins deserve
> or repaid us according to our offenses. (Psalm 103:8-10)

> Tear your hearts,
> not just your clothes,
> and return to the LORD your God.
> For He is gracious and compassionate,
> slow to anger, rich in faithful love,
> and He relents from sending disaster. (Joel 2:13)

God's compassion in these verses isn't what we normally think of as compassion; it is not simply reaching out to help someone in need. The Old Testament uses a particular Hebrew word to describe the compassion of God. The word is *racham*, and it's like a beautifully wrapped gift just waiting to be opened and explored. It means "compassion—as cherishing the fetus in the womb."[1] In other words, the way a mother feels about her unborn child—those feelings of deep love, nurture, and protection—are the same feelings God has toward us. Nearly every time this word *racham* is used, it is connected with God's extending love and mercy toward us when we deserve anger and punishment. Jesus came as the flesh-and-blood demonstration of the amazing compassion of God.

The disciple John told the story of a woman who found herself in the fight of her life. We don't know the beginning of her story; we only know that by the time she met Jesus in John 8, she had been convicted of adultery and was facing an angry mob of men ready to dole out justice via a good old-fashioned stoning. The text is clear: She wasn't just accused of adultery; she was caught red-handed. The case was closed and her fate was sealed.

I wonder if, as she faced her impending death, she was reliving and regretting the decisions that had led to that moment. Have you ever found yourself in a battle of your own making? Ever been entirely helpless to explain your way out of trouble and completely dependent on the mercy of people who want nothing more than to make you pay? That's this woman. Her life was over, her future was finished, and she was about to die a very painful, very public death.

But then came Jesus. He stepped into the story at the baiting of the Pharisees, who believed they had trapped Him in an untenable situation. Fifth-century church father Augustine succinctly summed up the problem Jesus faced: "If he shall approve her being stoned, he will not show his gentleness; if he consent to let her go, he will not keep righteousness."[2] Jesus did neither. Instead, He stooped and wrote we-know-not-what with His finger and then uttered words that have become iconic in our culture: "The one without sin among you should be the first to throw a stone at her" (verse 7). One by one, the oldest men began to peel away from the crowd while Jesus returned to the dirt. Don't you wish John had let us in on the secrets written there?

With every accuser gone (to buy flowers for their wives, perhaps?), Jesus, the only one qualified to throw a stone, demonstrated His Father's character of compassion with this death-defeating pardon:

"Woman, where are they? Has no one condemned you?"
"No one, Lord," she answered.

> "Neither do I condemn you," said Jesus. "Go, and from now on do
> not sin anymore." (verses 10-11)

The compassion of God, powerfully expressed through Jesus, stays the execution, holds back the rocks, and restores our future. The One who ruthlessly fights against our enemies also fights for our forgiveness and freedom.

I experience this aspect of His character nearly every day in my own life, especially in this season of battle. So many times I slip into fear of the future, and then I try to manipulate things into going my way, or I find myself stuck in a ditch of frustration and selfishness and I blame Him instead of blessing His name. Truth is, I get it wrong a lot, and I can't imagine how frustrating it must be for Him to watch me spinning my wheels, thinking I can do life without Him when He has already proven He is ready and able to care for my every need. Though He is right and I am wrong, He chooses to treat me with compassion. God's compassion doesn't ignore our sin but rather adds comfort to the correction and healing to the hurt, saying, "Go and sin no more."

The world and even the church sometimes paint an ugly picture of God as a volatile father waiting to backhand His kids as soon as they disappoint Him. Maybe you've experienced a father like that and so the image makes sense to you. But what if God isn't mad at you? What if He is, instead, pretty crazy about you and in love with the idea of helping you look more and more like His own dear Son (see Romans 8:29)?

The God Who Fights For You is good, kind, and slow to

anger. He does not repay our sin or screwups in ways we deserve.[3] Your sin has not disqualified you from seeking His help in the heat of battle. When you feel surrounded by accusers with rocks in hand, you can be certain that God is not one of them. Our good, compassionate God lavishes mercy instead of anger on all who ask (see Acts 2:21). Isn't that the best news ever?

More reading: Psalm 86:5,15; 103:1-14; 111:4; Joel 2:13; Ephesians 4:32; James 5:11

## WORTH PONDERING

1. Write about a time when you felt accused or judged.

2. List five words that describe Jesus' actions in this story. How have you experienced these aspects of His nature?

3. Do you or someone you know have a tendency to believe that God is mad at you? What do you think caused this misconception of His character?

## CHAPTER 4

## *The God Who Fights For You . . .*
# GOES BEFORE YOU

In my office hangs a sign that has become a lifeline to me throughout the course of our battle. Even though the sign has only two words on it, I read it every day—several times every day, in fact—and those words give me hope and strength to face whatever comes. The sign simply reads, "Every minute."

Soon after Steve's diagnosis, I was desperately listening for assurance from the Holy Spirit that I would survive this fight, and I distinctly heard Him say, "I've been to every minute you will ever face, and I've placed provision there. You won't see it now, but it'll be there when you get there." Sure enough, now three years into our battle, I can say with confidence that I have experienced in countless, convincing ways the very provision He promised. I no longer have any doubt that He began fighting ruthlessly for us long before we knew the giant of ALS was coming. This assurance amazes and comforts me daily.

Each of the following treasures from Scripture underscores

the truth that God is before all things. If you're the kind of person who writes in books, circle the words *begin, beginning,* and *before.*

> In the beginning God created the heavens and the earth. (Genesis 1:1)

> In the beginning [before all time] was the Word (Christ), and the Word was with God, and the Word was God Himself. He was present originally with God. All things were made *and* came into existence through Him; and without Him was not even one thing made that has come into being. (John 1:1-3, AMP)

> The LORD himself goes before you and will be with you; he will never leave you nor forsake you. Do not be afraid; do not be discouraged. (Deuteronomy 31:8, NIV)

> Behold, the former things are come to pass, and new things do I declare: before they spring forth I tell you of them. (Isaiah 42:9, KJV)

> [Earnestly] remember the former things, [which I did] of old; for I am God, and there is no one else; I am God, and there is none like Me, declaring the end *and* the result from the beginning, and from ancient times the things that are not yet done, saying, My counsel shall stand, and I will do all My pleasure *and* purpose. (Isaiah 46:9-10, AMP)

I am the Alpha and the Omega, the First and the Last, the Beginning and the End. (Revelation 22:13)

Before a word is on my tongue you, LORD, know it completely. (Psalm 139:4, NIV)

God has gone before all things. Before creation. Before time. Before you and before me. He has always been and will always be ahead of us, which positions Him to see our fight from a different perspective. We stand on the shifting sand of the temporary, but He occupies the richly *finished* space outside of time. He has a clear view of the beginning and the end. God goes ahead of us into battle, which should give us heaping helpings of courage. Here's why:

- If God goes first, He always knows what's coming, even when we don't.
- If God goes first, we never go anywhere alone.
- If God goes first, we can trust that He knows exactly which enemy is around the next corner and that He has the skills and resources to fight for us.
- If God goes first, we don't have to plot our own strategy or manipulate our own success; we only need to follow Him.
- If God goes first, we can trust that He has placed the provision we will need for the days we will face and we'll see it when we get there.

God is always ahead of us, and we can run as fast as our little legs will carry us, but we will never pass Him up. It is, however, possible to lag behind God or go in another direction from Him. David moved sideways when he slept with Bathsheba. Jonah left the beaten path when he purchased a ticket on a boat headed away from Ninevah. Though we sometimes disobey and sidestep God's will, He still calls us to turn our feet and follow. If we're wise, we'll trust His voice and make the turn.

The God who has always been first will always be first. And when we learn to trust that He is ahead of us, we'll begin to see His fingerprints all over the place. I have decided to follow Jesus, the One who goes first. Will you?

More reading: Deuteronomy 31:6; Joshua 3:6; Jeremiah 1:5; Micah 2:13; Colossians 1:15-17

## WORTH PONDERING

1. Think of the fiercest battle you have faced. Had you known then how the battle would turn out, how might you have fought or thought differently while it was in progress?

2. If you were convinced that God had gone before you into the battle you are facing right now (or into any you will ever face), how might it change the way you feel about the fight?

## CHAPTER 5

## *The God Who Fights For You . . .*
# SEARCHES FOR YOU

It's hard to imagine the God of the universe searching for something. I lose things all the time. In fact, my husband recently suggested that I could write a truckload of books in the time I spend looking for my keys every morning. Losing is easy. Finding is hard. But finding the lost is part of Jesus' mission statement: "The Son of Man has come to seek and to save the lost" (Luke 19:10).

In Luke 15, Jesus tells three search-and-rescue stories, and He tells them in order of escalating importance. First, a man with one hundred sheep loses one. That's only 1 percent of his flock, but the man still leaves the ninety-nine to find the one in danger. Next, a woman loses one of her ten silver coins, which is 10 percent of her treasure. She sweeps and searches until she finds it. Finally, a man loses his beloved son. This one son represents 50 percent of the father's legacy, but anyone who has lost a child understands that the son occupies 100 percent of the father's heart.

It's interesting that Jesus starts with two objects that bear little responsibility in the losing. A sheep is not smart and a coin is inanimate, so the reason they are lost is connected back to a mistake or negligence on the part of the owners. The third story, however, takes the analogy to a whole new level. A father doesn't lose a grown son. A grown son chooses to leave and disappear from his father's life. In this story, in fact, the son leaves willfully, knowing his actions shoot daggers through his father's heart. He doesn't just slip away; he storms out, carrying armloads of Daddy's cash, slamming the door behind him. Lost? Not by a long shot. Yet Jesus, who never loses anything, includes the prodigal son in these lost-and-found stories.

Let's jump back to our first verse out of Luke 19. We often read iconic verses like this one as isolated, stand-alone truth, but this verse is part of a bigger story, the story of a wee little man, a man who probably felt lost and invisible for much of his life: Zacchaeus. Here's the tale:

> He entered Jericho and was passing through. There was a man named Zacchaeus who was a chief tax collector, and he was rich. He was trying to see who Jesus was, but he was not able because of the crowd, since he was a short man. So running ahead, he climbed up a sycamore tree to see Jesus, since He was about to pass that way. When Jesus came to the place, He looked up and said to him, "Zacchaeus, hurry and come down because today I must stay at your house."
>
> So he quickly came down and welcomed Him joyfully. All who saw it began to complain, "He's gone to lodge with a sinful man!" (verses 1-7)

Zacchaeus was lost in sin. Tax collectors were the worst sort of swindlers, and he was a chief among them. I think he was lost in other ways too because a man too short to see over the heads of the crowd is surely used to being overlooked himself. His immediate response to Jesus' invitation makes me want to cry. He was clearly hungry for hope and redemption. He was hungry to be found. And when the crowd warned Jesus of guilt by association, Zacchaeus could have defended himself or hurled his own accusations, but he didn't:

> Zacchaeus stood there and said to the Lord, "Look, I'll give half of my possessions to the poor, Lord! And if I have extorted anything from anyone, I'll pay back four times as much!" (verse 8)

This is a man who knows he's lost, and he is begging Jesus for a road map to relationship. Jesus gives it:

> "Today salvation has come to this house," Jesus told him, "because he too is a son of Abraham. For the Son of Man has come to seek and to save the lost." (verses 9-10)

Today. Without preconditions or collecting IOUs Jesus welcomes Zacchaeus back like the shepherd welcomed the sheep, the woman welcomed the coin, and the father welcomed the runaway son. He didn't lose Zacchaeus, but He helped him find his way back.

It's easy to get lost. We, the ignorant sheep and rebellious sons, are prone to wander, but The God Who Fights For Us is a searching God. He is also a "Come to Me" God, meaning He won't violate our free will to get us to come to Him. But He will watch and call to us where we're hiding. His love seeks us out, calls us by name, pursues us through missteps and mistakes, and rejoices when we finally turn toward Home.

If the battle you face has made you feel lost and alone, if you've ever uttered the desperate words "Where is God? Why can't I find Him?" please know this: The God you are searching for in your darkest moment is searching for you. He is watching, loving, and looking toward you, and He sent His Son so you could be found, forgiven, and free.

Perhaps you are not wandering but you love someone who is. Oh, friend, please know that you serve a search-and-rescue God and He doesn't have to be begged or cajoled into a passionate pursuit of the lost. Those dearest to our hearts are even dearer to His, and we can count on Him to find them where they're hiding and offer them a way back to grace. He lives to seek and save. We are living proof.

More reading: Psalm 34:15; Proverbs 15:3; Jeremiah 29:14; Ezekiel 34:11-16

## WORTH PONDERING

1. What is the most significant thing you have ever lost? To what lengths were you willing to go to find it?

2. Have you ever felt like the least important person in God's world? What does the parable of the lost sheep tell you about your position in God's heart?

3. We see clear evidence that God searches for that which is lost. What might this mean for the battles that we feel are lost?

## CHAPTER 6

*The God Who Fights For You . . .*
# LOVES A GOOD PARTY

Few people would describe Leviticus as a "party book." It's filled with rules, regulations, and a seemingly endless array of punishments for those who violate them. It's austere and somber. It's definitely no Song of Solomon or Philippians. But for some reason, I've become rather fond of this book. My appreciation grew as I began to see through the rigid requirements and into the heart of God. He longs for relationship with His people. He aches to be near them, live in their space, and occupy their world, but He can't live alongside their sin, so Leviticus (and all the rules therein) creates a bridge between their humanity and His holiness. The Law was not intended to keep them out of relationship but rather to invite them in.

Looking at Leviticus as an invitation rather than an indictment, let's turn our attention to chapter 23. Read these verses and circle all the words that sound like a party:

The LORD spoke to Moses: "Tell the Israelites: In the seventh month, on the first day of the month, you are to have a day of complete rest, commemoration, and joyful shouting — a sacred assembly. You must not do any daily work, but you must present a fire offering to the LORD." (verses 23-25)

"You are to celebrate the LORD's festival on the fifteenth day of the seventh month for seven days after you have gathered the produce of the land. There will be complete rest on the first day and complete rest on the eighth day. On the first day you are to take the product of majestic trees — palm fronds, boughs of leafy trees, and willows of the brook — and rejoice before the LORD your God for seven days. You are to celebrate it as a festival to the LORD seven days each year." (verses 39-41)

These verses describe two festivals, but there were seven in all. The Israelites had seven events throughout the year for rest, remembering, eating, giving, blessing, worshipping, and celebrating. Some of the feasts were solemn and reflective. Others were wildly exuberant, involving the waving of lambs and wheat and bread. The feasts were beautiful because they brought the people's thoughts back to the miraculous ways God had fed and led them for generations. They served as a marker that fastened the hearts of the people back to the majesty of their Maker. God could have built these reminders around anything, but He chose these seven festivals.

The Bible gives clear evidence: God loves parties because He loves people. In fact, John tells us the story of Jesus' first miracle, which happened to take place at a party:

On the third day a wedding took place in Cana of Galilee. Jesus' mother was there, and Jesus and His disciples were invited to the wedding as well. When the wine ran out, Jesus' mother told Him, "They don't have any wine."

"What has this concern of yours to do with Me, woman?" Jesus asked. "My hour has not yet come."

"Do whatever He tells you," His mother told the servants.

Now six stone water jars had been set there for Jewish purification. Each contained 20 or 30 gallons.

"Fill the jars with water," Jesus told them. So they filled them to the brim. Then He said to them, "Now draw some out and take it to the chief servant." And they did.

When the chief servant tasted the water (after it had become wine), he did not know where it came from — though the servants who had drawn the water knew. He called the groom and told him, "Everyone sets out the fine wine first, then, after people have drunk freely, the inferior. But you have kept the fine wine until now." (John 2:1-10)

Every time I read this story, I marvel that Jesus chose this as His first miracle. Compared to healings and resurrections and such, it seems almost frivolous, but He cared enough to bring the best wine to that wedding. Jesus cared about this couple's party.

In fact, it seems that Jesus spent a fair amount of time sharing food with friends, and He didn't limit Himself to friends from church:

> While He was reclining at the table in Levi's house, many tax collectors and sinners were also guests with Jesus and His disciples, because there were many who were following Him. When the scribes of the Pharisees saw that He was eating with sinners and tax collectors, they asked His disciples, "Why does He eat with tax collectors and sinners?"
>
> When Jesus heard this, He told them, "Those who are well don't need a doctor, but the sick do need one. I didn't come to call the righteous, but sinners." (Mark 2:15-17)

The Pharisees have a point. For a guy claiming to represent God (see John 10:30), Jesus could have done something far more divine than pulling up a seat next to shysters and scam artists. But like His Father, Jesus meets us around the table of relationship. We could craft a lot of doctrinal reasons for His attraction to feasts and dinner parties and celebrations, but what if it's as simple as this: God loves to be with us, and He's glad when we show up.

My favorite party I've ever been to was my own wedding. My dress was big. My hat was big. My hair was big. But when I saw Steve for the first time that day, I didn't wonder if I looked okay. I didn't worry whether the flowers were the right shade of red. All I could see was joy: mine and his. I knew with my whole heart that no one had to convince him to marry me. In fact, the whole day was one big expensive party, celebrating the fact that Steve had found me and pursued me and that I had said yes. Steve was in that church on a snowy February morning with no reluctance. He showed up eagerly and joyfully.

God has the same joy toward us:

As a groom rejoices over his bride, so your God will rejoice over you. (Isaiah 62:5)

He has not been cajoled into coming for us. He comes with joy, He seeks us out with joy, and He rejoices over us with shouts of joy. Can you picture His seeing you and letting out a belly laugh because He's just so happy it's you and so glad you and He are together?

Sadly, the world lacks an authentic representation of our happy, celebrating God. As hard as it is to believe, the Bible declares that God is glad to see us. He's the father who raced to meet his wayward son in the driveway and instead of throwing a fit threw a party (see Luke 15:20). That's our Dad.

When people share their painful stories with me, they're often burdened and buckling beneath the weight of failure and sin. Sometimes we sin our way into battles and it's hard to believe that God would ever want to fight for us, to help us, much less throw a party for us. But what if we believed it? What if we absorbed this idea that God is not shaking His fist in scorn because we messed up again but is instead throwing wide His arms to welcome us back, with a deep laugh and shout of joy? That's the character of our beautiful, rejoicing God.

More reading: Hosea 14:4; Matthew 3:17; Luke 15:11-32; John 15:11; 17:13

## WORTH PONDERING

1. What is the best party you've ever been to? What made it so wonderful?

2. Write about a time when you felt that God was happy to be with you.

3. In what places or situations do you feel the presence of God most profoundly?

## CHAPTER 7

*The God Who Fights For You . . .*
# CANNOT BE COMPLETELY EXPLAINED

When I was in high school, the Rubik's Cube took the world by storm. I'm not good at puzzles, and after about two minutes of trying to line up all those silly colored squares, I usually flung it across the room, declaring it impossible. The first time I watched someone solve it, I was mesmerized (but still not interested in spending any more time trying to crack the code). Since then, many bigger, more-complicated puzzles have come along, especially in the world of technology. My kids understand computers in ways I never would have imagined when I was their age and the term *HTML code* lived only in the vocabulary of highly trained specialists. Now scientists have decoded so many secrets of the universe that we tend to distrust things we can't fully understand. It seems that virtually everything can be pulled apart, examined, and reconstructed.

Everything, that is, except God. While I believe that God

can be known and His character is clearly revealed through the Bible, my humanity will always prevent me from comprehending the full magnitude of His divinity this side of eternity.

When we find ourselves in a Big Battle, however, the stuff we can't explain about God can become a sticking point. For instance, I see many places in the Bible where the power of God brings physical healing to the sick. Believe me, these stories and verses have been sent to me in countless cards and notes since Steve's diagnosis. I absolutely believe that God heals, and I've even experienced His healing personally, yet God hasn't healed Steve.

This could be a point of contention in my relationship with Him, but I'm comforted by the words of Job, who went ahead of me on this battlefield. God showed up and took Job to school for shaking his fist at the heavens and demanding answers for the unrelenting suffering in his life. The scene takes place over four chapters (see Job 38–41), with God asking question after question, insisting that Job take a good look at all the things he did not and could not ever know. It was a stunning display of God's power (and proves that He invented sarcasm). At the end of it all, Job concluded,

> I'm convinced: You can do anything and everything.
>> Nothing and no one can upset your plans.
> You asked, "Who is this muddying the water,
>> ignorantly confusing the issue, second-guessing my purposes?"
> I admit it. I was the one. I babbled on about things far beyond me,
>> made small talk about wonders way over my head. (42:1-3, MSG)

If I'm ever going to know anything about God's character with certainty, I must be equally certain that some things about Him will always be beyond my finite, fragile understanding. When I don't know the answer to a question such as "Why does God heal some people and not others?" I remember that God is mystery and I lean hard on the things that I *do* know.

I know He fights for me, ruthlessly.

I know He is good, always.

I know He goes before me.

I know He wins. Always.

I know that when I get to heaven, I will owe Him everything and He will owe me nothing.

And this is enough for me. It may seem like taking the easy way out theologically, but I assure you that nothing about this battle is easy. When our experience seems to conflict with the promises of the Word, it's hard. It's painful. But our commitment to trust God stands when He outperforms our expectations, and it also stands when He does not and life is not as we thought it would be. I will trust Him without conditions, without apology, and without regret. What I do know is enough to hold my faith steady through the storms that are caused by what I don't know.

The apostle Paul many times talked about his calling to make known the mysteries of God (see Ephesians 3:4; Colossians 4:3), but he also reiterated the words of Isaiah from Isaiah 40:13:

Oh, the depth of the riches
both of the wisdom and the knowledge of God!

How unsearchable His judgments
and untraceable His ways!
For who has known the mind of the Lord?
Or who has been His counselor?
Or who has ever first given to Him,
and has to be repaid?
For from Him and through Him
and to Him are all things.
To Him be the glory forever. Amen. (Romans 11:33-36)

Although we will spend our lives diving into the truths of His character that can be known, we must also get comfortable with the magnificent mystery of His ways. The corners we can't see or imagine, the aspects of His image that don't even have names yet, the infinite dimensions of His love—this is what it means to know the Uncreated One. We, the creation, will never understand Him completely, and that's not just okay, it's beautiful. Any god that could be contained by a mind as small as mine would not be big enough to trust with my eternity.

Sometimes, in the dark of night, I dream of the moment I will stand before Him in heaven, knowing as I am known. I imagine that in the beauty of all things revealed, I will only be able to stammer out the final summation of my friend Job: "I had heard rumors about You, but now my eyes have seen You."

More reading: Romans 11:33-36; 1 Corinthians 2:6-9; 13:12; 1 Timothy 3:16

## WORTH PONDERING

1. What do you feel is the most mysterious thing about God?

2. In what ways does the mystery of God affirm His magnitude?

3. Write down three things you know to be true of God. How might you hold to these in the midst of the unknown?

## CHAPTER 8

## *The God Who Fights For You . . .*
# LISTENS TO YOU

On a busy day long ago, I pushed a towheaded, talkative three-year-old through a crowded store while I tried to come up with dinner ideas as she asked question after question (after question). She kept asking and I kept nodding and murmuring autopilot Mom responses, thinking I was fooling her into believing I was engaged in the conversation. Finally, she tired of fighting for my attention and said, "Mom, I need you to listen." Without stopping, I said, "Honey, I am listening." She reached a chubby hand up to hold my face and gently moved it toward her, saying, "I need to *see* you listen." Busted.

All of us long to be truly known and undeniably heard, but in our mile-a-minute world, it seems harder and harder to get anyone's attention. Social media has created a noisy push-and-shove arena in which only the strong, successful, or shocking can be heard above the clamor of the crowd. So many voices fill our planet, each one longing for someone to listen with their eyes and ears and all their hearts.

Take a look at this:

The eyes of the LORD are on the righteous, and his ears are attentive to their cry. (Psalm 34:15, NIV)

I call on You, God,
because You will answer me;
listen closely to me; hear what I say.
Display the wonders of Your faithful love,
Savior of all who seek refuge
from those who rebel against Your right hand. (Psalm 17:6-7)

The God Who Fights For You is not closeted away in a cloudy, cotton home; He is positioned at the threshold of trouble, and He is near enough to hear your cries for help. In fact, in Psalm 38:9, King David says that God even hears our sighs. It's such a gift to know that the God who is the author of all words would care about hearing mine. I long for Him to hear me when I'm in trouble, when I'm lonely, when I need help, and the Bible assures me He can and does hear me. This is great news. If He is the God who hears, then I am the kid who is heard. And so are you.

God hears our worship, our prayers, our dreams, and our cries for help in battle. He hears every word we say to Him. However, He also hears us when we're talking *about* Him. Here's what Moses said to the children of Israel as they grumbled their way through the wilderness:

> You will know that it was the LORD when he gives you meat to eat
> in the evening and all the bread you want in the morning,
> because *he has heard your grumbling against him.* Who are we?
> You are not grumbling against us, but against the LORD.
> (Exodus 16:8, NIV, emphasis added)

Sobering, isn't it? It seems that God's attentiveness is so complete and sincere that it extends to all our conversations, questions, and complaints, not just those directed at Him.

I recently caught myself saying some weak words on a weary day. Discussing a difficult decision we were making, I murmured to a friend something along the lines of, "This would be a really good time for God to show up with an answer." As soon as the words left my lips, I knew they had been heard and regret rolled over my aching heart. I knew that my strong God—the God who has not left my side for a moment of this battle—was listening as I accused Him of showing up late to my fight. I wondered about the millions of times every day when He is maligned or misjudged by the words of those who claim to know and love Him.

Knowing that God is listening makes me want to use words in better ways. I know it's always safe and right to be honest with Him, but a new understanding of this aspect of His character has produced a fresh desire to speak in life-giving, God-honoring ways, even in the middle of the battle. He is listening. I am heard. This is wonderful, indeed.

More reading: Psalm 38:9; 65:2; 94:9; Proverbs 15:29; Isaiah 59:1

## WORTH PONDERING

1. Who is the best listener you know? How does that person's attentiveness make you feel?

2. In general, how often do you speak to God in the course of a day? How about when you are in a fierce fight?

3. How would your prayer life change if you were absolutely, positively convinced that God hears every word?

*The God Who Fights For You . . .*
# ALWAYS WINS

When I first began to study all the battles in the Bible, my goal was to uncover as many principles as possible about the surprising beauty found in a fierce fight. The most significant truth that emerged was simply this: When God fights, He wins. Every time. He doesn't go easy on His opponent in order to make the loser feel better. He doesn't try to level the playing field. He doesn't give the bad guy a head start. He wins—fiercely, unapologetically, and often violently.

We see this when the Israelites were fleeing from the Egyptians, who were in hot pursuit of them, and God fought ruthlessly on Israel's behalf by leveling the Egyptians with a little weapon of war called the Red Sea. Another time He caused the walls of Jericho to come tumblin' down, destroying the city in one fell swoop. He also ruthlessly defended His people against the Assyrians (see Isaiah 36–37), the Amalekites (see 1 Samuel 30), and a large band of camel-riding Midianites (see Judges 6). When God is involved in the battle, everybody doesn't get a trophy.

But this is ancient Old Testament history. How does this aspect of God's character play out in an era when, instead of Goliath, Sennacherib, and Pharaoh, our enemies have names like Fear, Shame, and Depression? Oh, fear not, good soldier. Your battle has already been ruthlessly fought and decisively won by the Son of God.

Whenever I read the story of the crucifixion, I cringe at the brutality of it all. This was not a civilized execution; it was a cruel, drawn-out, excruciating, and merciless killing. As the body of Jesus was violently destroyed, Satan had to be thinking, *I'm winning! I'm winning! I'm winning!* But when Jesus breathed His last breath, the earth shook and the veil split, and that's when the real winner took the stage. Read this one out loud, triumphantly:

Having disarmed the powers and authorities, he made a public spectacle of them, triumphing over them by the cross. (Colossians 2:15, NIV)

And because it's especially awesome, check out Eugene Peterson's translation in *The Message*:

That old arrest warrant canceled and nailed to Christ's cross. He stripped all the spiritual tyrants in the universe of their sham authority at the Cross and marched them naked through the streets.

The beautiful present-day, post-Cross truth is that Jesus has already fought death and won for us. He didn't lose against His enemies, and He won't lose against ours.

In the battles of the Bible, we find that sometimes people—even God's people—decide to go to war without Him. Sometimes their disobedience lands them in a pickle, and they arrive in a land that can only be described as Losing. Have you felt the sting of losing? I have. I've been known to pick the wrong fight and march off without Him, thinking He's mad at all the same people I'm mad at. This never ends well. An essential part of knowing the God Who Fights For Us is knowing when to fight, when to forgive, and when to wait for His clear direction. But when, like David when he marched against Goliath, we know that our enemy is also God's enemy, then we can say with confidence that the battle is the Lord's (see 1 Samuel 17:47).

Battles are scary, and when I am in the middle of one, I'm often tempted to plot out a strategy or devise a clever Plan B in case God doesn't show up in time. But the more I get to know the Battle God of the Bible, the more I trust Him to deal ruthlessly with my enemies in His way and time. In the end, He will win. He always does.

More reading: Psalm 18; Isaiah 37:33-38; Ephesians 1:20-23

## WORTH PONDERING

1. How would you react if a knife-wielding stranger came against your child or someone you love?

2. Have you ever used the word *ruthless* to describe God? Why or why not?

3. How might a fresh understanding of God's ruthless nature aid you in the battles you face?

## CHAPTER 10

## *The God Who Fights For You . . .*
# NEVER GOES MISSING

I often turn to the book of Psalms for encouragement, but every once in a while, I run into a doozy of an opening line, like this one:

> LORD, why do You stand so far away? Why do You hide in times of trouble? (Psalm 10:1)

Have you ever felt as if God has gone missing from your life? I have. This psalmist did, and he gives voice to the words hidden in many of our hearts. But this view of God is not at all in line with the character of God. He never leaves us. He is always near. Read this good news:

> The LORD is near the brokenhearted; He saves those crushed in spirit. (34:18)

And look at this one:

> God is our refuge and strength, a helper who is *always found* in times of trouble. (46:1, emphasis added)

Artists can paint portraits of a God who keeps humanity at arm's length, but their portraits of Him are incorrect. In our dog-eat-dog world, it's easy to feel that we need to keep our best foot forward and try to clean ourselves up before we come to Him. But God is as near as our broken hearts (see 34:18) and He moves toward our suffering, not away from it. He created us for relationship, and even when we run and hide, He longs to be close to us.

In the first chapter of Matthew, the angel appears to Mary to announce the impending arrival of the Messiah. I wonder if all of heaven held its breath when Gabriel got to the part where he told Mary that the baby's name would be "Immanuel, which is translated, 'God is with us'" (Matthew 1:23). God's very name speaks of His character.

It was Christmas time when I was eight months pregnant with our fourth child, our son. As I set up my favorite nativity set, I placed the baby Jesus in the beautiful little stable and thought how cozy His world looked. He had a fluffy hay bed surrounded by adoring shepherds and His very own angelic host. A strong dad, a beautiful mom, and even a few pleasant-looking animals completed the lovely scene. But as I sat there, dreaming of the coming of God's son, He reminded me of the soon-expected arrival of mine. I went to the room that would be Josiah's nursery, looked around at soft blankets and tiny clothes, and felt a holy whisper to my heart, "Imagine when Josiah is born that I asked you to take your only son, place him in his car seat, and leave him in a city dump in a faraway country. He will grow up there and be one of them. He will live like they live and eat the scraps they eat, and he will spend his days telling the people in the dump that his parents have a home with land and a kitchen and three square meals a day. He will tell them that there is life outside the dump. They will listen, some will be intrigued, but eventually they'll grow weary of his talking and they'll take him and kill him. In his very last moments, he'll call out for you, but even you will turn away from your one and only son."

Tears rolled as the story played out in my mind and, for the first time ever, I had a small understanding of the four incredible words "God is with us." God in our broken, battered world. God in our poverty and pain. God in the dump we call home, coming to meet us and mend us and remind us that there is a better home waiting.

The book of Matthew is bookended with this principle of God coming near and staying near. In the last lines of the gospel, Jesus says these parting words to the disciples: "And remember, I am with you always, to the end of the age" (28:20). Oh, I do love that word *always*; it reaches all the way from the disciples on that day to me on this day, to my children and to my children's children on every day that will ever come. The evidence that God is committed to close proximity with us is irrefutable and overwhelming.

I know how easy it is to feel alone on the battlefield. But when you know the character of The God Who Fights For You, you know that alone is not possible. He will never go missing. He loves to be with you, meets you in your messiest moment, and will never leave you on your own. It's His character and it's His name.

More reading: Joshua 1:5; Psalm 46:7; Daniel 3:22-25; Matthew 5:4; Hebrews 13:5

## WORTH PONDERING

1. Think of a moment when you felt alone. Where do you think God was during that time?

2. Think of a moment when you felt near to God. Why do you think you felt His presence so strongly in that moment?

CHAPTER 11

*The God Who Fights For You . . .*
# COVERS AND CARRIES YOU

I was raised before car seats were mandatory for small children. Instead of a car seat, I had a protective mother who possessed a lightning-fast, right-arm-extension reflex whenever she was behind the wheel. Regardless of who was on the seat beside her, she would immediately throw that arm out to prevent her passenger from experiencing harm. My mom did everything she knew to do to keep her kids safe. (Nowadays we know it was a terrible strategy, but not then.) And as I've been studying the character of God, I've discovered He does the same. My mom's stubborn refusal to let harm come to her children is a direct reflection of our dear Father.

God is fiercely protective. Scripture speaks of this character trait many times. The Bible writers continually reassure us of two facts of life: (1) We will experience trouble, and (2) we can count on God's protection when we do. Although He doesn't always keep us out of our enemy's line of sight, He does offer a strong, protective arm when the bad guys get too close. Look at these words from Psalm 91, perhaps one of the most-memorized chapters in the Bible:

> The one who lives under the protection of the Most High dwells in the shadow of the Almighty. (verse 1)

> He will cover you with His feathers; you will take refuge under His wings. His faithfulness will be a protective shield. (verse 4)

> Because he is lovingly devoted to Me, I will deliver him; I will protect him because he knows My name. When he calls out to Me, I will answer him; I will be with him in trouble. I will rescue him and give him honor. (verses 14-15)

Along the same line, David wrote these amazing words about the protective refuge of God:

> I say to the LORD, "You are my God."
> Listen, LORD, to my cry for help.
> Lord GOD, my strong Savior,
> You shield my head on the day of battle." (Psalm 140:6-7)

> You, LORD, will guard us;
> You will protect us from this generation forever. (12:7)

Did you catch that? Read that last verse again, out loud. How long does God promise to protect His own? *Forever.* Amazing.

More than ten centuries later, Jesus claimed this promise of protection for those He loves as He spoke to His Father on the eve of His crucifixion:

> I am not praying that You take them out of the world but that You protect them from the evil one. (John 17:15)

A few years later, the apostle Paul echoed Jesus' words:

> The Lord is faithful; He will strengthen and guard you from the evil one. (2 Thessalonians 3:3)

In His faithfulness, God covers and carries us when harm comes our way. He stands as our shield in danger, our refuge in war, and our guardian in chaos. If our immediate instinct is to shield our children from trouble, how much more protective is our great God, who sees our battle from every angle? He knows the fearsome landscape of the world in which we live, and He goes with us into every situation as our ever-present safety and defense.

Some nights when I lay in bed feeling exhausted and over-whelmed by the battle at hand, I focus my thoughts on this part of God's nature. I roll these verses through my mind and give myself permission to fall into the safety of His love. I remind myself that I am the kid and He is the Father. And unlike my mother's, His arm really *is* strong enough to save.

More reading: Psalm 69; 71; 91

## WORTH PONDERING

1. Do you believe that feeling protected goes along with feeling loved? Why or why not?

2. Is there something or someone over which you are protective? How far would you go to keep that thing or person safe?

3. Do you ever find it difficult to let someone else take care of you, as though maybe it's irresponsible or weak? Take a minute to think of ways you could invite the protective love of God into your battle today.

## CHAPTER 12

*The God Who Fights For You . . .*

# KEEPS GOOD BOOKS

Our world is rife with injustice.

In 1992, after several police officers were acquitted in the beating of Rodney King, racial tensions boiled over in Los Angeles. Angry mobs took the law into their own hands, and fifty-three innocent people died when they were caught in the crossfire of this violent cry for "justice."

I recently talked with a woman whose husband left her after decades of marriage. He had spent several years hiding money and assets, strategically untangling their life together while pretending to still love her. When he left, she found herself suddenly alone, broke, and homeless. Her longing for financial and emotional justice is almost palpable; it consumes her.

My husband and I are privileged to serve on the board of a home for AIDS-affected orphans in Nairobi, Kenya. Kings Kids Village[1] houses, feeds, and educates forty kids who represent the most vulnerable demographic on the planet, and each has a backstory of tragic injustice. I'm so glad they are safe now, but for each KKV kid finding hope and a home, there are a million more orphans who are not.

Let the record show: We live in an unfair world. I'm sure you have some records of your own. But God is not blind or deaf to our need. In fact, the Bible makes it abundantly clear that The God Who Fights For Us loves and does justice. Here's just a fraction of the evidence:

> The mighty King loves justice. You have established fairness; You have administered justice and righteousness in Jacob. (Psalm 99:4)

> Righteousness and justice are the foundation of Your throne; faithful love and truth go before You. (89:14)

> Preserve justice and do what is right, for My salvation is coming soon, and My righteousness will be revealed. (Isaiah 56:1)

As in each of these verses, the Bible consistently connects God's righteousness and justice like links on a chain. In his book *The Character of God*, R. C. Sproul states that "God is at once righteous and just. The two concepts are so closely connected that, though they can be distinguished, they cannot be separated."[2]

The word *righteous* relates to conformity to God's standard. Righteousness,[3] then, is what God believes about right and wrong. He created all things rightly positioned for unbroken relationship with Him and in harmonious relationship to one another. But when sin sent us spinning, we lost our moral bearings and have struggled ever since to pinpoint what we believe about right and wrong. God, however, has never wavered, and His righteousness has not budged one iota. He is always right.

God's justice[4] is demonstrated in the actions that flow from His righteousness. These just acts are essentially the "verdict" in a case, punishing wrongdoers (see Romans 1:18) but also offering rights to the vulnerable or victimized (see Psalm 140:12). It's impossible to have complete justice unless it is rooted in complete righteousness. Even in a society built on a strong axis of justice, we're sometimes going to get it wrong. As in the case of the Rodney King riots, our humanity sometimes drives us to seek vengeance in place of justice. How can our limited understanding accurately pinpoint the line between punishment and revenge? The moment the penalty exceeds the crime, a new injustice has been committed.

The same limitations apply when we're working to defend the rights of the helpless. Though we can, and should, work to achieve a better life for widows, orphans, and the disenfranchised in our world, we can't possibly heal all the wounds injustice has caused. Only a God who sees all, knows all, and has access to supernatural resources can be trusted to execute righteousness and justice for every person of every race, gender, and social status.

After hearing countless battle stories, I've concluded that most battles can be traced back to an injustice of some kind. People are often unkind, unfair, and unfaithful, and we bear the scars of their missteps and mistakes. And when there's no bad guy to blame, it can seem that God Himself has been unjust. But that isn't possible. He would have to violate His own righteous nature, and He will never do that. What do we do, then, when it seems we're the victims of injustice, and God has not shown up to defend our cause or plead our case? The answer is found as we shift our perspective from this temporary trouble and fasten it on heaven, our permanent home. One man helped me learn this lesson well.

My father-in-law served God faithfully until his death in 2013. Paul Stern was famous for his unstoppable faith in the purposes of God and was nearly impossible to rile up. He was so confident in God's ability to work every tough situation out in the end that he just did not worry about much of anything. When he suffered a wrong, he would often smile and say, "Don't worry. God keeps good books." This attitude held him strong and steady through some of the hardest seasons in his life. It kept him joyful in suffering and patient in battle. At his funeral, kids and grandkids, friends and coworkers could be heard quoting that classic Paul Stern line to one another. We would laugh through our tears knowing that Paul was finally experiencing the fulfillment of that promise.

My father-in-law maintained a living, active understanding that God is just and that even if we don't see it here on earth, we'll see it in eternity. I believe it. I am certain that our good God will wipe every tear and right every wrong. He will heal every disease and welcome every orphan into His embrace. From His righteousness will flow endless streams of justice and joy. I can hardly wait to see it.

More reading: Psalm 50:6; 82:3; 111:7; Proverbs 21:3; Jeremiah 17:10; 2 Thessalonians 1:6

## WORTH PONDERING

1. What is the most serious injustice you have suffered or witnessed? How has it impacted your view of God's justice?

2. Have you ever stepped in to defend the cause of someone being treated unjustly? What was the result?

3. Journal your thoughts about how righteousness is essential for true justice to flow. How would this look in the battle you are facing?

## CHAPTER 13

*The God Who Fights For You . . .*
# MAKES YOU MIGHTY

When I was little, my friends and I often played the game loosely titled "My Dad Is Stronger Than Your Dad." It went something like, "My dad is so strong, he can move the couch by himself." "Oh yeah, well my dad is so strong he can move the piano!" Back and forth, back and forth, until the game was trumped by the dad who could lift the entire planet and all of the objects in it, past, present, or future. We all want to have a strong dad, and most men hope to be strong dads.

This has been a tender topic in my home over the past two years as my husband who once defined the word *strapping* has watched his muscles slowly, steadily deteriorate. ALS destroys motor neurons, and no one knows why. Healthy motor neurons move our muscles into action, so when they stop working, our muscles think they're no longer necessary and give up. Steve's muscles are giving up, and it seems as though he loses a bit more of his strength every day. At first that meant I had to open the mayonnaise jars on my own; now it means I have to help him dress and lift the spoon to his lips during meals. The man who used to bench-press well over two hundred pounds can no longer pull the covers up over himself at night.

It's hard to watch someone I love live without strength. That's why this aspect of God's character is so magnificent to me. He is strong. Our Dad is stronger than any other human, power, or principality. But the really big deal here is this: Not only is He very powerful but He's also willing to share His strength with others. Most particularly, He shares His strength with the weak. Read this:

"Even so, be strong, Zerubbabel" — this is the LORD's declaration. "Be strong, Joshua son of Jehozadak, high priest. Be strong, all you people of the land" — this is the LORD's declaration. "Work! For I am with you" — the declaration of the LORD of Hosts. "This is the promise I made to you when you came out of Egypt, and My Spirit is present among you; don't be afraid." (Haggai 2:4-5)

Therefore I was left alone, and saw this great vision, and there remained no strength in me: for my comeliness was turned in me into corruption, and I retained no strength. (Daniel 10:8, KJV)

He said, "Don't be afraid, you who are treasured by God. Peace to you; *be very strong!*" As he spoke to me, I was strengthened and said, "Let my lord speak, for you have strengthened me." (Daniel 10:19, emphasis added)

He said to me, "My grace is sufficient for you, for power is perfected in weakness." Therefore, I will most gladly boast all the more about my weaknesses, so that Christ's power may reside in me. (2 Corinthians 12:9)

Read that last verse again, out loud. *Asthenes*, the Greek word translated here as "weakness," means "ailments, diseases, infirmities, weakness."[1] In general, it speaks of the conditions of our humanity that create disabilities. That's bad news. But here's the great news: *Dunamis*, the Greek word translated here as "strength," means "ability, might, miraculous power, strength."[2] Isn't that exciting?

I am seeing the fulfillment of this Scripture in my husband's life. I am watching the ability of God come into his disability. God's might is overwhelming Steve's weaknesses in ways that cause him to be stronger in spirit, purpose, and vision than he has ever been before. I know many who would say that the only acceptable outcome for Steve's life is miraculous, physical healing, but I am seeing miraculous strength invade his being in ways that can only be supernatural. He is physically weak, but he is being made gloriously strong by the God who is willing to share His power with those who most need it.

In fact, this is true of our whole family. Had you asked me three years ago how we would handle a giant of this magnitude, I wouldn't have known what to say. Now my answer is definite: God has made us mighty. He has given us strength not just to stand but to reach out to others who are suffering. He has filled us with purpose and blessed us with credibility inside a community we didn't know about before our own battle with ALS. We now share His love for the many families dealing with this disease, and love never fails. It always makes us stronger than we were before. I hope it makes those who receive it stronger as well.

When a Really Big Battle lands on the doorstep, it's tempting to flex our muscles and hope we can duke it out and win. But as I look more intently at the character of God, I see that He is waiting, willing, and excited about showing Himself strong *for* us and *through* us. First Peter 5:10 is one of my favorite go-to verses right now. Earlier in the book, Peter tells us that the Enemy is on the prowl, looking for ways to dismantle and destroy us. He's on a mission and we are his target, and that sounds scary to a weak girl like me. But then I read 1 Peter 5:10:

> After you have suffered for a little while, the God of all grace who called you to His eternal glory in Christ will Himself restore, confirm, strengthen, and establish you. (NET)

The God of grace wants to bring His strength to our weakness, His power to our pain, His muscle to our fight. Let's let Him.

More Reading: 2 Samuel 22:18; Psalm 18:17-18; 2 Corinthians 13:4

## WORTH PONDERING

1. What do you typically do when you feel that your strength is depleted?

2. Write about a time when you felt overmatched by an issue, a person, or a problem.

3. How easy or difficult is it for you to believe that the strong God who goes before you into battle is willing to share His strength for your fight?

## CHAPTER 14

# *The God Who Fights For You . . .*
# CREATES CONSTANTLY

Days after my first child was born, I nearly called the doctor because I was certain something was wrong with my neck. Then I realized it was just sore from staring down at that baby, hour after hour, day and night. Children so fresh from God are astounding; their tiny beings brilliantly display His creative abilities. So does Niagara Falls. And outer space. And the deep, blue sea. And the mountains surrounding my city. And sunsets, snowflakes, and tree frogs.

There is no end to God's design. His majestic creativity is written in skies, stones, and the sounds of a symphony. The longer I live and the more I see, the more I begin to understand that His artistic abilities are limitless.

The Bible affirms God's creative nature from beginning to end:

God created man in His own image;
He created him in the image of God;

He created them male and female. (Genesis 1:27)

How countless are Your works, LORD!
In wisdom You have made them all;
the earth is full of Your creatures.
Here is the sea, vast and wide,
teeming with creatures beyond number —
living things both large and small. (Psalm 104:24-25)

Everything was created by Him,
in heaven and on earth,
the visible and the invisible,
whether thrones or dominions
or rulers or authorities —
all things have been created through Him and for Him.
(Colossians 1:16)

Whenever the living creatures give glory, honor, and thanks to the One seated on the throne, the One who lives forever and ever, the 24 elders fall down before the One seated on the throne, worship the One who lives forever and ever, cast their crowns before the throne and say:

Our Lord and God,
You are worthy to receive
glory and honor and power,
because You have created all things,
and because of Your will
they exist and were created. (Revelation 4:9-11)

That last verse stuns me. I don't often fall down on my face before God, worshipping Him because of all that He has made. Clearly, the citizens of heaven understand something I have not yet grasped. From their angle, viewing the vast expanse of a universe crafted as a home for the children of His love, worship is the only response. I'd like it to be mine, too. I'd like to wake up every morning focused entirely on what God has created and not on what the Enemy has tried to destroy. It would be silly for me to try to convince you that this is always easy. You know it's not. When a battle rolls through your formerly peaceful life, it can feel that you're losing everything. Everything. Sometimes my only hope for staying steady in the fight is to shift my weight from the tumultuous battlefield and lean hard into the things that are not being shaken or taken. This is not a random, sporadic exercise for me. It's daily and intentional and involves an actual list of the things He has created that remind me of His character:

- I have an eternal inheritance. (So do you!)
- I have the unconditional love of the God who is for me, not against me. (You, too!)
- I have a beautiful world. (My world is surrounded by the Cascade Mountains. What surrounds yours?)
- I have an army that loves me. (Who's in your army?)
- I have hot coffee in my favorite cup. (What's in your cup today?)
- I have love to give and purpose to live. (I'm praying as I write this that you know you have this too.)

It may seem unnaturally regimented and forced to read a list, but I do it every day because the results are supernatural. As I wake up my spirit to the creative power of God by reminding myself of what He has already done, I have faith to face whatever this battle brings. I am sometimes tempted to move into the ditch of self-pity and despair and stay there, but I don't because I know He has created me for more. I want to live wonderstruck by His power and skill. Our God is a creative genius, and we are His best work. It's a wonder too great for words.

More reading: Psalm 8; Isaiah 43:6-7; 54:16-17; Ephesians 2:10

## WORTH PONDERING

1. What is the best thing you've ever created?

2. Read Ephesians 2:10. How easy or difficult is it to believe that the same God who made the wonders of the world made you?

3. If you truly believed that God has the power to create, Satan has some power to destroy, but God has the power to re-create, how might it change the way you face your battles?

## CHAPTER 15

# The God Who Fights For You...
# DOES NOT CONDEMN YOU

One common denominator I have found among people fighting hard battles is that most of them, at one time or another, have been annoyed by the words of their well-meaning friends. Often it's not the actual words that bother them; it's the fact that those giving advice are sitting safely on the sidelines and, therefore, do not fully comprehend the suffering taking place on the battlefield. I understand this one. Those traveling the dark roads of the valley of the shadow of death do not love being told what to do by those who seem to be living on Easy Street.

This is one reason I love the books written by the apostle Paul: They are words *for* the battlefield, written *from* the battlefield. Paul experienced beatings, stonings, shipwrecks, and hunger, and many of his letters were written from a prison cell. His suffering makes him a credible counselor, and his words give hope, encouragement, and correction to those who feel alone or abandoned in the fight. Take a look at this:

> What, then, shall we say in response to these things? If God is for us, who can be against us? (Romans 8:31, NIV)

Paul makes a bold assertion: God is not against us. He's not trying to catch us doing something bad, and He's not watching to make sure we get everything right before He blesses us.

God is *for us*. He fights FOR us. He fights for US. It's too wonderful to comprehend. And Paul goes on to explain how *much* God is for us.

> He who did not spare his own Son, but gave him up for us all — how will he not also, along with him, graciously give us all things? (verse 32, NIV)

He's for us to the degree that He sacrificed Jesus in our place. He saw our wretched, rotten, willful sin and sent His perfectly beautiful, entirely holy Son to die so we could live. He sent Him so we could have *all things*. Amazing. So why is it hard for us to really believe that God is for us? The next verse gives a clue:

> Who will bring any charge against those whom God has chosen? It is God who justifies. Who then is the one who condemns? (verses 33-34, NIV)

Ah, see it there? We have an enemy. And it is the fervent desire of our enemy to make us believe that we are not good enough for God to love—that we are not accepted by Him because we are not right enough or holy enough or fixed enough. Satan brings the charge and instead of recognizing the assault of our enemy, who is always, always out to kill, steal, and destroy (see John 10:10), we question the grace of God. We wonder if it extends as far as we have drifted. We fear we are out of reach. And when those doubts drift in, when we feel unworthy, it's natural to wonder why God is so hard to please. Our enemy will try to manipulate us into questioning our Father's innate goodness, but he doesn't have the power to bend our thinking away from truth unless we give it to him. Paul asks, "Who is the one who condemns?" and the immediate answer is:

> No one. Christ Jesus who died—more than that, who was raised to life—is at the right hand of God and is also interceding for us. (Romans 8:34, NIV)

Even when we doubt His love, even when we're swayed by the accusations of our enemy, God is still for us. Interceding. Advocating. Loving us to new life.

The next part of Paul's declaration played over and over in my head on the day Steve was diagnosed with ALS. A friend had texted it to me earlier that morning, and it weaved and bobbed through my questions as we drove the three hours home from our doctor's office. It wrapped itself around my confusion. It spoke through the tidal waves of fear that inevitably swelled when I thought about what our future held. Paul's words became a mantra for me. They proclaim the testimony of God's character, and, even in those desperate moments, I knew that even ALS could not wedge its foot in the door between God's love and me.

> Who shall separate us from the love of Christ? Shall trouble or hardship or persecution or famine or nakedness or danger or sword? As it is written:
>
> "For your sake we face death all day long;
> we are considered as sheep to be slaughtered."
>
> No, in all these things we are more than conquerors through him who loved us. (verses 35-37, NIV)

This I know: God is for us. Three years later, I could not be more certain of it. This disease is not a sign that He's condemned us or a test to see if our faith can stand in the fire. God is with us and fights ruthlessly for us. His love has had the last word on every dark day. Because of that, I don't just read the final words of Paul in Romans 8; I own them. I breathe them. I live them.

> I am convinced that neither death nor life, neither angels nor demons, neither the present nor the future, nor any powers, neither height nor depth, nor anything else in all creation, will be able to separate us from the love of God that is in Christ Jesus our Lord. (verses 38-39, NIV)

More reading: 1 Kings 8:57; Psalm 56:9; Isaiah 50:7; 1 Corinthians 1:30

## WORTH PONDERING

1. Write about a time when you felt condemned by others or by God.

2. How easy or difficult is it for you to believe it when Paul says that God is *for you*? Explain your answer.

3. How might the landscape of your battle change if you really believed that the God of the whole universe was on your team?

## CHAPTER 16

*The God Who Fights For You . . .*

# KNOWS YOUR NAME

My son's fifth-grade teacher was an excellent math instructor. He was good at resolving conflict and was a great blend of tough and fair. However, from the first parent-teacher conference in September to the last one in June, he struggled to remember Josiah's name, regularly calling him the very wordy "Joseph—I mean, Josiah!" We ran into him at the park a few weeks after school ended and, sure enough, he smiled and exclaimed, "Joseph!" It's hard to feel known or cared for by someone who doesn't even know your name. Our names are the starting point of all the other knowing.

Even though I'm convinced God has infinite knowledge and understanding of all the details of the universe, it's still so significant to me that He knows my name. He knows how I became Bo Stern and all the meaning my name holds for me. Even with all the children He has to remember, He knows exactly who I am. We live in a world where people forget our names or don't even bother to learn them, and that makes this verse so dear to me:

> Don't be afraid, I've redeemed you.
>> I've called your name. You're mine.
> When you're in over your head, I'll be there with you.
>> When you're in rough waters, you will not go down.
> When you're between a rock and a hard place,
>> it won't be a dead end —
> Because I am GOD, your personal God,
>> The Holy of Israel, your Savior.
> I paid a huge price for you: . . .
>> That's how much I love you!
> I'd sell off the whole world to get you back,
>> trade the creation just for you. (Isaiah 43:1-4, MSG)

Here's another verse, written to unfaithful Israel, yet teeming with life and beauty:

> Look, I have inscribed your name on my palms; your walls are
> constantly before me. (Isaiah 49:16, NET)

What does it mean that God has inscribed the Israelites' names on His hands? Bible scholars disagree on the details, but most concede this one thing is certain: God has written the names of His children in a place where He will always see them and will never forget them. To *inscribe* means "to cut in." To engrave. When we buy a new leather Bible, we engrave our name on the cover to show that the Bible belongs to us. I find it amazing that God did something similar with the Israelites. He engraved their names on His hands, showing ownership, affection, and His deep awareness of their identity as His children. He saw their ruined walls, collapsed by the consequences of their own sin, but He also saw their original identity and all they were created to be. His decision to inscribe their names into His hand had nothing to do with their worthiness and everything to do with His love for them. One more promise, from the lips of Jesus Himself, so you can see that this name-knowing characteristic of the Father is also the character of the Son, our Savior:

> The sheep hear his voice. *He calls his own sheep by name* and leads them out. . . . The sheep follow him because they recognize his voice. They will never follow a stranger; instead they will run away from him, because they don't recognize the voice of strangers. (John 10:3-5, emphasis added)

Doesn't it seem odd that He would talk about a shepherd knowing the names of the sheep? I can imagine him knowing their weight and coloring and tendency to wander and all sorts of other things, but I cannot imagine that the sheep have names. Yet, Jesus uses this example to show us a picture of relationship. Those sheep are similar in so many ways, but their shepherd knows them individually and personally. He doesn't beckon them as a group, He calls each one. By name.

Josiah's teacher happened to be with his two sweet young sons on the day we ran into him at the park. He introduced them to us, and he got their names right the very first time. They are his sons; he knows them. If he were to get a tattoo, it would not be the name of a student but rather the names of the children who belong to him. You belong to your Father. Say your name out loud. That very name was written with nails in the palm of His hand. That very name is written in His book (see Revelation 3:5) and is dear to His heart. Have you ever felt lost in the swirling crowds of people? Does it seem as though your name tag has faded into obscurity and no one has noticed that it is missing? Take a minute to listen for the voice of the Great Shepherd today. *Your* shepherd. He's calling for you, and He's calling you by name. No matter how many are in His care, He will not forget you, and He will always fight for you.

More reading: Psalm 139; Jeremiah 1:5; Revelation 3:5

## WORTH PONDERING

1. What importance do you give to remembering people's names? Is it important to you that others remember yours? Why or why not?

2. Write down the meaning of your name. Does it reflect your character? Why or why not?

3. Have you ever felt "called by name"? How did that moment impact your life?

## CHAPTER 17

# *The God Who Fights For You . . .*
# KNOWS YOU INSIDE AND OUT

If you've ever felt you needed to be on your best behavior with God, and if you're weary of hiding away the weak stuff in your life in order to keep your best foot forward, Psalm 139 is for you. King David launches this psalm with seven powerfully perfect words:

Lord, You have searched and known me. (verse 1)

Before moving on, read the verse out loud seven times, emphasizing a different word each time.

Now what do you feel? When I do this, my emotions run the gamut from gratitude to fear. On the one hand, I long to be truly seen and known, but on the other hand, being completely known is a frightening proposition. I know what lives in the closets and compartments of my life that no one else can see.

The real me is sometimes much less worthy than the one I try to show the watching world. My motives veer wildly between virtuous and villainous, so maintaining a little distance between my inner mess and the Godhead seems wise. So I hide the ugly stuff and push the more pleasing parts of me to the surface. Accomplishments move to the top of my résumé, highlighted, italicized, and underlined; failures are buried deep in the footnotes.

Yet, down in the depths of my heart, where my secret dreams, fears, and insecurities hide, I live with the sneaky suspicion that it's impossible to be unconditionally loved without first being completely seen and known. So I wonder, *What if? What if it is possible to be truly seen and truly known and still, somehow, utterly and entirely loved?* And what if that seeing and loving was done by an impossibly beautiful Friend?

According to King David, that is the case. He wrote,

> You know when I sit down and when I stand up;
> You understand my thoughts from far away.
> You observe my travels and my rest;
> You are aware of all my ways.
> Before a word is on my tongue,
> You know all about it, LORD.
> You have encircled me;
> You have placed Your hand on me.
> This extraordinary knowledge is beyond me.
> It is lofty; I am unable to reach it. (Psalm 139:2-6)

I agree with David: The knowledge that I am completely known *and* completely loved is too wonderful. My thoughts cannot capture or contain it. God sees every detail, from my wild successes to my deepest sin and sorrow, and loves me in spite of all my messes and mistakes. God's love searches for me, calls me out of hiding, and assures me that it's safe to be broken in front of Him. It's right and good to need grace.

David's words invite us to throw back the curtains and welcome the sunlight of God's searching into our souls, even though it will undoubtedly reveal some grease and grime.

> I will praise You
> because I have been remarkably and wonderfully made.
> Your works are wonderful,
> and I know this very well. (verse 14)

The One who made us knows us and *loves us*; He loves every single particle of us and invites us to acknowledge the grandeur of His workmanship. Read the first line again:

> I will praise You *because* I have been remarkably and wonderfully made. (emphasis added)

May I paraphrase this verse for you? "God, I worship You because Your work in my life is amazing. Astounding. Remarkable! In spite of all I am not, You love and adore what I am."

God does not roll humans off His assembly line like Barbie dolls at a factory. He fashions each soul individually, carefully (see Ephesians 2:10), and then goes before us and behind us as we travel through life. He watches and works everything together to mold us into the image of His own dear Son (see Romans 8:28-29) because His plans for us are infinite, individual, and intimate. Take a minute now to consider that the God who knows you completely and loves you outrageously also knows every detail of the battle you face. Now, doesn't that make you feel strong for the fight?

More reading: Isaiah 43:1-5; 49:16; Jeremiah 1:5; Luke 12:7; John 10:3; Revelation 3:5

## WORTH PONDERING

1. "LORD, You have searched and known me" (Psalm 139:1). What is most difficult for you to believe about those seven words?

2. In what ways has God shown that He knows you?

3. In what ways has He shown that in spite of knowing you so well, He still loves you unconditionally?

## CHAPTER 18

*The God Who Fights For You . . .*

# GIVES GOOD DIRECTIONS

A few years ago, I spoke at a conference in Seattle, a city I had loved from afar but never explored. On the last day of my trip, I found myself alone with a rental car, a GPS, and an afternoon to kill, so I set out to find a great cup of Pacific Northwest coffee and a fun place to shop. Well, after lots of driving and looking and "recalculating," I ended up drinking Starbucks at a sad little strip mall. Though I had a GPS that could get me anywhere I wanted to go, it couldn't tell me *where* I wanted to go. I didn't know the city, and the GPS didn't know me, so instead of discovering Seattle, I got stuck in the suburbs.

My dear friend Pam lives near Napa Valley and knows the area very well. She also knows *me* very well. When I went to visit her there, she met me at the airport, itinerary in hand. She knew exactly where we would go, where we would eat, what we would see. She had planned the trip to maximize every minute we had to spend and to do the things she knew I would most want to do, and it was the best adventure ever.

We often treat God like a GPS, but He's really much more like a friend who rides in the car with us. He knows every inch of the road ahead and He knows us, so He is able get us where He wants us to go (and makes the trip more fun, too!). Life is filled with big crossroads moments, such as deciding who to marry, choosing a career path, and navigating a dark road with a dear child. Being confident in God's willingness to lead and guide is essential for making good decisions and avoiding costly mistakes. It's His character to lead us safely, but sometimes it's hard for us to believe it.

I've talked with so many women who are worried or doubtful about finding the will of God for their lives. Some of them even seem to view it as a mean-spirited game God plays with humans. Crack the secret code, and we eventually arrive in the magical, mysterious land called Our Destiny; misread the map, and we end up on a long, lonely detour. But God is not trying to trick us; He wants us to know His will. The Bible tells us so:

> I will instruct you and show you the way to go; with My eye on you, I will give counsel. (Psalm 32:8)

> You did not abandon them in the wilderness
> because of Your great compassion.
> During the day the pillar of cloud
> never turned away from them,
> guiding them on their journey.

And during the night the pillar of fire

illuminated the way they should go. (Nehemiah 9:19)

I love the way Paul says it in Romans 8:28:

We know that all things work together for the good of those

who love God: those who are called according to His purpose.

*Prothesis*[1] is the Greek word translated here as *purpose*, and it means "a setting forth" or a "proposal." The purpose to which we are called is His plan for our lives. It's not just a destination; it's an itinerary that includes all the places we will go as His grace leads us. In God's sovereignty, He knows where to take us in order for us to experience full joy and satisfaction in our handful of days here on earth. Because He loves us, God wants to be our tour guide on the trip.

That's not to say that it's always easy to hear Him clearly and obey completely. I'd love to tell you there's a secret formula for downloading God's entire plan for you in advance, but that's not the way it works. God gives good directions, yes, but He often gives them step-by-step. Look at the instructions He gave to the Israelites as they prepared to march in to battle for their Promised Land:

When you see the ark of the covenant of the LORD your God, and

the Levitical priests carrying it, you are to move out from your

positions and follow it. Then you will know which way to go,

since you have never been this way before. (Joshua 3:3-4, NIV)

Before the Israelites could know which way to go, they had to move toward God's presence. That one step of faith positioned them for the next one and the one after that. Over and over in Scripture, we see that God leads us as we move in faith:

Your eyes will see your Teacher, and whenever you turn to the right or to the left, your ears will hear this command behind you: "This is the way. Walk in it." (Isaiah 30:20-21)

The path of the righteous is like the light of dawn, shining brighter and brighter until midday. (Proverbs 4:18)

Having walked this far through this fight, I can tell you that there have been plenty of days when I have not been able to see the path ahead clearly, and by "clearly" I mean "at all." Illnesses like ALS come packaged up with a seemingly endless array of weighty decisions, many of them with the power to impact everything from our finances to our kids to the number of Steve's days. I'm not smart enough to know what to do, so my first response is usually to panic. When that fails to produce results (again), I remember that I don't need to be smart; I just need to listen and obey. As soon as I move my eyes off the heat of the battle and back to my faithful Leader, the path begins to come into view. Sometimes it's the right Scripture at just the right time or an e-mail from a friend or just the supernatural peace of God that floods our hearts as we take a step in the way we feel Him leading. As we focus on the character of the One who gives good directions, we have the faith and assurance we need to take the next step. He has never failed to guide us safely into His will.

No matter how big the fight you face today and no matter how you got there, believe that God is always willing to lead you to security and peace. Shift your vision away from the tumult of battle and fill your heart with His presence and His Word, confident that He gives good directions to those who ask.

More reading: Psalm 1:6; 25:14; Isaiah 26:7; Colossians 1:9-10

## WORTH PONDERING

1. Think of a time when you felt lost. What was your first response?

2. If you had the opportunity to see the entire plan for your life in advance, would you take it? Why or why not?

3. If you were certain God would lead you safely to His will, how would it change the way you fight the battles you face?

CHAPTER 19

# *The God Who Fights For You . . .*
# LONGS FOR YOU

I have longed for many things in life. I longed for the Malibu Barbie Dreamhouse (never got it). I longed for a cutting-edge video game called "Pong" (got it!). I longed to go to college, longed for friends, longed to marry a good man, longed for children, longed for food, longed for vacation, and most recently longed desperately for a cure for ALS. I've never met anyone, no matter how privileged they've been in this life, who is unfamiliar with longing.

Would it surprise you to discover that God is no stranger to longing? Couldn't God, who created the universe with just a word, snap His fingers and immediately fill any desire in His heart? Makes sense in theory, but the Bible does not support this idea theologically.

Let's look at three distinct instances of God-longings. First, Isaiah paints this beautiful picture of a waiting, longing God:

The Lord [earnestly] waits [expecting, looking, and longing] to be gracious to you; and therefore He lifts Himself up, that He

may have mercy on you *and* show loving-kindness to you.
(Isaiah 30:18, AMP)

God created us with a desire for the very thing He longs to give us: grace. We, a people starving for grace, happen to have a Father who longs to give just that. Doesn't that seem like a match made in heaven and a perfect scenario for joy?

Second, Jesus expresses this same longing in the gospel of Luke:

Jerusalem, Jerusalem, you who kill the prophets and stone those sent to you, how often I have longed to gather your children together, as a hen gathers her chicks under her wings, and you were not willing. (Luke 13:34, NIV)

I love the language here. Jesus longed to throw His arms around His children and keep them wrapped in His promise of salvation like a mom throws a warm quilt around a shivering child. He longed to cover and carry them. But they refused. (I've often been the hard-to-carry kid myself.)

The third instance of God-longing appears in Luke 22. Jesus knows His days are numbered and He gathers His dearest friends around Him for a meal. We fancy this passage up with religious language and symbolism, but look at the way Jesus describes His heart to His friends:

When the hour came, He reclined at the table, and the apostles with Him. Then He said to them, "I have fervently desired to eat this Passover with you before I suffer. For I tell you, I will not eat it again until it is fulfilled in the kingdom of God." (Luke 22:14-16)

Jesus *fervently desired* to eat with His friends. To remember Passover. To share a meal and conversation and time. He wasn't punching the relationship clock; He longed for their company before He suffered. The Bible is clear: Jesus loves relationship with us. He wants to spend time and share life with us. Being with Him is not about checking a box on the Bible reading plan so He won't be mad; it's about the mutual communion and companionship that happens in a friendship.

My family gathers every Sunday evening for a big dinner. We laugh and dance to silly '80s music and argue and eat copious amounts of food. It's noisy and messy and the best part of my week. I look forward to these gatherings with those who are dearer to me than anything in this world. As my husband lives in the shadowy valley of a terminal diagnosis and a two-to-five-year prognosis, none of us takes our time together lightly. We all show up. We have a better understanding of Jesus' fervent longing to eat with His friends "one last time" than we used to. Jesus longs to be with us. It's an amazing and humbling and beautiful truth.

These three passages show us that God longs for something only we can provide. All His longings are tied to us. He doesn't just put up with us or reluctantly redeem us; He saves us because He loves us and longs to be with us, now and forever, so much so that His longing drove Him out of heaven and into our world. For God so loved and longed for us, that He gave. And gave. And continues to give. Isn't that too marvelous for words?

More reading: Read Song of Solomon 7:10 in as many translations as you can find, and then write your favorite rendition out on a sticky note to put in a place where you'll see it often. Remember each time that you are the object of His fervent longing.

## WORTH PONDERING

1. Close your eyes and consider this question: What is the deepest longing of your heart?

2. Knowing that you are the deepest longing of God's heart, how might that change the way you turn to Him in times of battle, discouragement, or weariness?

3. Write the following on a sticky note and place it somewhere you'll see it each day: "I am my Beloved's, and His desire is for me."

## CHAPTER 20

*The God Who Fights For You . . .*
# SHARES YOUR SUFFERING

I have been so blessed to have a veritable army of amazing people fighting for me in the course of our battle with ALS. They're all a great gift, but two of them are uniquely positioned to offer something the others cannot. Linda's husband, John, was diagnosed with ALS six years ago, so she has lived on this battlefield twice as long as I have. Libby's husband, Jack, was diagnosed at nearly the same time as Steve, but the disease progressed very rapidly and he died within eighteen months. Both Linda and Libby provide insight into my fight and wisdom for the tasks and decisions that go along with this battle. But beyond the information we give one another about life with ALS, we share a connection that is powerful and important even if no words are spoken.

Libby called me recently, on the one-year anniversary of Jack's death. It was also the day my husband's first wheelchair was delivered. It's difficult to articulate the importance of our conversation as we entered the sacred space of shared suffering. We spoke of the tension between joy and sorrow and the ways wheelchairs help maintain independence. We talked about how Libby handles loneliness, and mostly we talked about gratitude. Over and over again, our words moved back to the faithfulness of God and the grace that is beyond our comprehension but essential to our survival. Had someone else called me on this particularly tough day in my fight and admonished me to be more thankful, I might have dismissed it as a platitude. But Libby's words carried a great deal of weight and immense credibility. People who have experienced suffering and are still filled with faith are like gold when we face a battle.

Jesus is such a friend. Though He was God, He was no stranger to suffering. In fact, one of His names is the Suffering Servant. Jesus didn't live tucked away behind the safety of His Father's protection; He came to our world and experienced life as we know it. He came not only to reach and teach us but also to suffer with us. In case you think maybe you've experienced something no one could ever understand, read these verses out loud:

In *all* their suffering, He suffered, and the Angel of His Presence saved them. (Isaiah 63:9, emphasis added)

He was despised and rejected by men, a man of suffering who knew what sickness was. (53:3)

Jesus tasted the bitter tears of affliction. Every affliction. From emotional rejection to the worst kind of physical torment to bearing the weight of every sin, Jesus has been there. His experience with suffering uniquely qualifies Him to meet us in ours:

> Since He Himself was tested and has suffered, He is able to help those who are tested. (Hebrews 2:18)

> We do not have a high priest who is unable to sympathize with our weaknesses, but One who has been tested in every way as we are, yet without sin. (4:15)

Have you noticed how often people tend to apologize for crying, as if crying is a weakness and sorrow is the opposite of strength? Worse yet, some people treat expressions of sorrow like the sure sign of a spiritual deficiency or lack of faith. But Jesus experienced every sorrow, and knowing this serves as a tether to pull us in tightly to His presence, comfort, and love. He doesn't resent our need for His help in times of suffering; He understands it and welcomes it. Let's read that last verse again, but add the verse that follows it:

> We do not have a high priest who is unable to sympathize with our weaknesses, but One who has been tested in every way as we are, yet without sin. *Therefore* let us approach the throne of grace with boldness, so that we may receive mercy and find grace to help us at the proper time. (verses 15-16, emphasis added)

Because Jesus is intimately acquainted with the pain caused by the battles we face, He is also infinitely qualified to meet us, heal us, and fight for us. His love invites us into the shared space of suffering, and it's on that common ground that the good news of the gospel comes alive. Jesus tasted death so we don't have to. His work on the cross paid the price for our eternal freedom so we can say with confidence that suffering is difficult but temporary. I'm so thankful for the God who understands every story and is aware of every sorrow. He can be trusted with our pain and will eventually turn our tears into a chance to dance (see Psalm 30:11).

More reading: Read Isaiah 53 out loud. It's a beautiful portrait of the Suffering Servant.

## WORTH PONDERING

1. What is the least-helpful advice you have ever received when you were suffering?

2. Write about something you have suffered that many people would not understand. How might it draw you closer to the comfort of Jesus?

3. How have the things you've suffered given you credibility to encourage someone else?

## CHAPTER 21

*The God Who Fights For You . . .*

# MAKES LITTLE INTO MUCH

We live in a never-enough sort of world. With multitudes of people crowding into our survival-of-the-fittest society, it can seem as though all of life is a zero-sum game. Your win means less for me. My loss is more for you. Is it any wonder we brutalize one another for the right to control our planet's dwindling, finite resources? And if we live this way with our material possessions, it stands to reason that we would do the same with our emotional resources as well. We are not just starving for wealth; we're starving for significance. And that's a deeper issue because it moves us beyond the weedy ground of Not Having Enough and plants us firmly in the rugged wilderness of Not Being Enough.

The God of the Bible, however, lives entirely outside the game. Into our never-enough world, He brings a more-where-that-came-from abundance. Here's proof. These verses are from different Bible stories, but they share a striking similarity:

The LORD asked him, "What is that in your hand?" "A staff," [Moses] replied. (Exodus 4:2)

Elisha asked her, ... "What do you have in the house?" (2 Kings 4:2)

[Jesus] asked them, "How many loaves do you have?" (Mark 6:38)

God fashions big and beautiful stuff out of small and inadequate supplies. From the staff in Moses' hand, He created an instrument of authority and security. Imagine how Moses felt holding that staff in his hand after pointing it at the Red Sea and watching the waters roll back (see Exodus 13–14)! Elisha's story shows us how an impoverished widow's desperation drove her to seek a miracle to keep her sons from being sold into slavery. In God's hands, the widow's small bit of oil became an unending supply that bought freedom for her sons and hope for their future. And from a paltry little lunch, Jesus created a meal for thousands and a miracle for the disciples to hold on to when their faith faltered.

These stories sketch the picture of a God who loves, loves, loves to take the little and make it much. The most impressive picture of His abundant resourcefulness, however, is what He did with a handful of dust and a spare rib.

The LORD God formed the man out of the dust from the ground and breathed the breath of life into his nostrils, and the man became a living being. (Genesis 2:7)

> Then the LORD God made the rib He had taken from the man into
> a woman. (verse 22)

The human race, created from the insignificant substance at hand. When God created everything else in the world, He did so *ex nihilo*— "out of nothing." Why did He vary from this pattern when it came time to create man and woman? I propose that He did so because He wanted us to know that although we are small, we are *something*. And our "something" can be transformed and brought to life by His breath and then used for His glory. Apparently (and awesomely!), this always-creating, always-upgrading characteristic is something He's willing to share with us:

> [Jesus] replied, "Because you have so little faith. Truly I tell you,
> if you have faith as small as a mustard seed, you can say to this
> mountain, 'Move from here to there,' and it will move. Nothing
> will be impossible for you." (Matthew 17:20, NIV)

I know I am small. And in the face of an Everest-sized battle, my faith often seems smaller than small. But God does not reject my too-little faith. Instead, He breathes His strength into the seed and allows me to share the thrill of His supernatural resourcefulness.

In a world that relentlessly reduces us to skin and bones, our God speaks abundant, outrageous life. He creates. He renovates. He turns trash into treasure, fish into a feast, and a nearly invisible grain of faith into a mountain-moving force. He speaks, and beauty grows wild on our battlefield, causing giants to fall and joy to rise. He moves, and hope runs loose through broken dreams, breathing life where death once danced. He is the God of more-than-enough. Believe it.

More reading: Genesis 1; Luke 16:10; 2 Corinthians 4:7

## WORTH PONDERING

1. In what area of life do you feel most in need of God's multiplying resourcefulness?

2. Think of a time you have seen God take something inadequate and use it for something glorious. What did this teach you about His nature?

3. On a scale of mustard seed to mountain, how big is your faith for the battle you face? Now is a good time to ask Him to turn your little to much.

## CHAPTER 22

*The God Who Fights For You . . .*

# DEFEATS DARKNESS

It happened at the Super Bowl in New Orleans in 2013. Just after Jacoby Jones returned the second-half kickoff 108 yards for a touchdown, the stadium went dark. And quiet. Seventy-six thousand people were, for a moment, immobilized, wondering who or what had caused the sudden darkness. And do you know what *didn't* happen when the lights went out? Football. You can't play if you can't see the ball, so the game stopped for thirty-four minutes while an undoubtedly frantic crew of technicians worked to fix the power problem.

Light is essential to life. It brings clarity and safety. It reveals beauty, and it illuminates danger and obstacles, enabling forward motion. In the eighth century BC, Isaiah wrote these words:

> The people that walked in darkness have seen a great light: they that dwell in the land of the shadow of death, upon them hath the light shined. (9:2, KJV)

Hundreds of years later, having witnessed the life, death, and resurrection of Jesus firsthand, Matthew was certain Jesus was the fulfillment of Isaiah's prophecy. When he quoted the prophet, however, the disciple changed two words:

> The people which *sat* in darkness saw great light; and to them which *sat* in the region and shadow of death light is sprung up. (Matthew 4:16, KJV, emphasis added)

Isaiah used the active words *walked* and *dwell*, but Matthew used the word *sat*. Theologian Frederick Dale Bruner believes that this change on Matthew's part was no mistake. The disciple was explaining that Israel was not just doing business as usual, hoping that someday a Savior might show up and restore their government. They were paralyzed without Jesus and desperate for His light to dawn. Without the arrival of the Messiah, the nation would have remained stuck in the ditch of unfaithfulness, repeating the patterns of a life lived in darkness.

> In Matthew's reading, they are so far in the dark that they cannot even move. . . . In Matthew's opinion the nations and even (unfaithful) Israel are in paralysis until Jesus comes to them; they sit enshrouded in night until Jesus' sun rises. The NT picture of the world without Christ is not bright; it is shadowy.[1]

I agree with Matthew, not because I know a lot about life in the eighth century BC or life in the first century, but because I know about life in the twenty-first century. It is dark without

Jesus. But we don't have to live in deep, paralyzing darkness. Our Savior has come, and He is Light and Life. The disciple John opened his gospel with a bright-light bang:

> In the beginning was the Word,
> and the Word was with God
> and the Word was God.
> He was with God in the beginning. . . .
> Life was in Him,
> and that life was the light of men.
> That light shines in the darkness,
> yet the darkness did not overcome it. (1:1-2,4-5)

I believe that John used these words at the beginning of his gospel to prepare us for what will happen at the end of his gospel: the crucifixion. On the cross, Jesus took on our fight with death and darkness, and darkness could not, cannot, will not ever snuff out the Light of Life.

Jesus came to free us from the fear of the shadowlands—of being swallowed up by the darkness of discouragement, doubt, and depression. He is Light, and He banishes darkness. The Cross opened up access to salvation, hope, and darkness-dousing light. When the battle feels overwhelming and it seems the night will never end, I cling to this truth of God's character: He came to bring unending, unquenchable Light. Weeping lasts for a while, but joy—and the sunrise—comes in the morning.

More reading: Isaiah 60; John 1:8-9; 2 Corinthians 4:6; Ephesians 5:8-13; 1 John 1:5-7

## WORTH PONDERING

1. List any areas in your life where it seems like the lights have gone out.



2. Take a moment and invite His light into those areas. Ask Him to illuminate all that you need to see and know to set your situation ablaze with His glory. The promise of the Cross is this: Darkness will not overcome you. This is as certain as the sun coming up tomorrow. Count on it.

## CHAPTER 23

*The God Who Fights For You . . .*
# GIVES YOU REST

I recently joined several coworkers at a two-day corporate training event focused on the development of individual vision and mission statements. With the help of a top-level business coach, we narrowed the scope of our lives, love, and work into a list of key core values. I've done similar exercises before, but this time it had fresh meaning because the battle my family has been facing for the past few years has redefined my priorities. When I finished writing down the third and final core value on my list, I saw evidence of the realignment that's taken place in my life. It read, "I value the healthy, holy rhythm of work and rest." I have always loved work. I was made for work. But I've not been good at rest. In fact, I've sometimes lived in fear of rest.

When Steve and I were newly married, I used to be afraid to sleep on road trips while he was at the wheel. I felt certain he needed me to be awake so I could alert him to any danger, and in various, annoying ways, I faithfully executed my duties riding shotgun. One day he gently reminded me that he had been driving for many years without my help and could probably handle it on his own from now on. I've realized I often treat God the same way. I act as if He needs me to toss and turn and stay awake through a crisis, thinking of all that could go wrong or hatching plans to fix a problem.

When I began to study His character in earnest, however, I discovered a God who has a strong work ethic and an equally strong rest ethic. God cares — really, really cares — that we get enough sleep, and He doesn't need us to stay awake, micromanaging His work.

> He will not allow your foot to slip;
> your Protector will not slumber.
> Indeed, the Protector of Israel
> does not slumber or sleep. (Psalm 121:3-4)

> Unless the Lord builds a house,
> its builders labor over it in vain;
> unless the Lord watches over a city,
> the watchman stays alert in vain.
> In vain you get up early and stay up late,
> working hard to have enough food —
> yes, He gives sleep to the one He loves. (127:1-2)

In our production-based society, it's hard to remember that the same God who placed Adam and Eve in the garden to work and run it (see Genesis 1:26) also commanded rest (see Exodus 31:15). But He did, because He knows we need it in order to thrive. Experts tell us that lack of sleep can cause wrinkles, forgetfulness, depression, and weight gain. Sleep deprivation also has negative effects on our sex lives and judgment and increases the risk of serious health problems such as heart attacks and strokes.[1] God knows how much we need to down-shift, especially in seasons of battle when we feel always on red alert, always trying to stay on top of the fight. Ironically, rest is often hardest to find in the moments we need it most.

If ever there was a season when I should have a hard time sleeping, it's this one. Sometimes the demands of the future creep in to haunt me in the night. In addition, Steve sleeps with a machine that sounds an alarm when his breathing grows shal-low, and every time it blasts through the dark silence, I wonder if I'm losing him. In the beginning, I thought the answer was to avoid sleep altogether. When my heart rolled with fear or anxiety, the last thing I wanted to do was turn off the lights and get in bed. It seemed easier to choose laundry or reading or television than quietness. But God has proven to me that He loves giving rest. It shuts me in with Him. There in the dark silence, I've learned to focus on His character and love. I replay the words He has spoken and remind myself of His mercy in my life. I remember that my husband is also God's dear son and that He loves Steve more than I ever could. I don't need to keep Him awake at the wheel. He is watching us and caring for us, so I can sleep in peace.

Though I know the scope of the battle we face, nighttime has become the sweetest part of my day, filled with meditation and gratitude. I'm convinced that when we learn to shift our fear and frustration into God's keeping and let Him bring peace to our turmoil, we grow stronger in battle and in life:

> When you lie down, you will not be afraid;
> you will lie down, and your sleep will be pleasant.
> Don't fear sudden danger
> or the ruin of the wicked when it comes,
> for the LORD will be your confidence
> and will keep your foot from a snare. (Proverbs 3:24-26)

"Pleasant sleep" does not seem synonymous with life on the battlefield, does it? Yet, God promises it. He promises that if we will focus on His goodness and trust in His power to save us, we can sleep without fear. How do we do that? The only answer I have is the one that's working for me: by setting our thoughts on Him. As we move our thoughts away from all that could go wrong and settle them on the strength, mercy, and endless love of God, we are able to find peace.

When I am overwhelmed and anxiety threatens to steal my sleep, it's so good to remember that God has already promised to provide it. He loves rest and is committed to giving it to His people in every season they face.

More reading: all of Psalm 4, which is called a night prayer; also Leviticus 26:6; Psalm 16:7; Proverbs 6:22

## WORTH PONDERING

1. How much do you value work? How about rest? Have you assumed that God values one more than the other?

2. Write about a season of battle when you felt that sleep was hard to come by.

3. How might a fresh understanding of the God who gives rest strengthen you for your fight?

## CHAPTER 24

# *The God Who Fights For You . . .*
# CAN BE TRUSTED COMPLETELY

Take a moment to think about the people you love. If you'd like, write down their names. Now think about the people whom you trust with your life. If the chips were down, if a Really Big Battle was on the horizon, who would you call first? Who would you call after that?

Sometimes we think love and trust go hand in hand, but I'm guessing the lists you just made are not the same. I love my sweet grandson, Greyson, more than almost anyone in the world, but I wouldn't call him if my house were on fire; I would call someone whom I knew had the skill, strength, and resources to douse the flames.

God can be trusted with your battle. He is *always* trustworthy. It's His character to be trustworthy. Read these verses out loud, emphasizing the italicized words:

The works of His hands are truth and justice; all *His instructions* are trustworthy. (Psalm 111:7)

*The decrees* You issue are righteous and altogether trustworthy. (119:138)

The instruction of the LORD is perfect, renewing one's life; *the testimony of the LORD* is trustworthy, making the inexperienced wise. (19:7)

The word of the LORD is right, and *all His work* is trustworthy. (33:4)

These verses tell us that God's instructions, decrees, testimonies, and work are all trustworthy. One hundred percent. Reliable beyond the smallest shadow of doubt. All that He does is strong, sturdy, and unfailing.

Over and over again in the Bible, we see that God uses the difficult situations in the lives of those who love Him to help them learn to trust Him. He asked Noah to build the ark and endure his neighbors' mocking long before He sent the first drop of rain (see Genesis 6–7). He asked Abraham to trust Him with the life of Isaac, his only child (see Genesis 22). Rather than stocking a storehouse full of manna, He sent it fresh every morning, giving the Israelites the chance to trust Him for daily bread (see Exodus 16).

God could have kept Noah, Abraham, and Moses from the situations that tested their faith, but He chose instead to teach them trust through them. In the course of my own battle, many people have offered the assurance that "God will never give you more than you can handle." I appreciate the sentiment, but I don't agree. Throughout the Bible and in my own life, I'm finding that He often allows us to encounter situations far beyond our own ability so that we will learn to trust His ability and His love.

On my bedroom mirror hangs a quote from Civil War chaplain E. M. Bounds. I cannot begin to tell you how many times I have recited this quote in order to remind myself of the character of God. Oh, how I love and cherish these trust-building words:

> When we pray, "Give us this day our daily bread," we are, in a measure, shutting tomorrow out of our prayer. We do not live in tomorrow but in today. We do not seek tomorrow's grace or tomorrow's bread. They thrive best, and get the most out of life, who live in the living present. They pray best who pray for today's needs, not for tomorrow's, which may render our prayers unnecessary and redundant by not existing at all! True prayers are born of present trials and present needs. Bread, for today, is bread enough.
>
> Bread given for today is the strongest sort of pledge that there will be bread tomorrow. Victory today is the assurance of victory tomorrow. Our prayers need to be focused upon the present. We must trust God today and leave tomorrow entirely with Him. The present is ours; the future belongs to God. Prayer is the task and duty of each recurring day — daily prayer for daily needs.[1]

No matter how fierce the fight or how long the night, He is the only One worth trusting when the chips are down. He will never fail or forsake you. The God Who Fights For You can be trusted with the details of your life, your love, and your battles. Trust Him.

More reading: Psalm 9:10; 73:28; 115:11; Proverbs 3:5; Isaiah 26:3-4; Romans 8:28-29

## WORTH PONDERING

1. Who is the most trustworthy person you know? Why?

2. What issue or person in your life is most difficult to give over to God's care?

3. How might your life change if you were truly willing to place that person or thing fully into His care?

## CHAPTER 25

*The God Who Fights For You . . .*
# KNOWS EVERYTHING

One day shortly after Steve's diagnosis, I hit an emotional breaking point. Waves of grief and fear washed over me, and I felt as though I were suffocating in a sea of sorrow, about to be swept under. I called my sister, desperate for help and hope, but all I could do was hold the phone and sob. Not knowing what to do or say next, she just sobbed too (oh, I'm so thankful for the people who share this battleground with me!). We cried out wordless prayers, and I know that God heard them because in just a moment, my brother-in-law came on the line. He said just a few words, but they have been a lifeline I have held on to for all the days since. "God's got this," he said, "and He's got you." Just that. *God's got this.*

The assurance I received from those words was this: God is brilliant beyond my comprehension. He's already been to the future and back, and He's holding every moment just as He holds every star. He's holding every tear just as He holds the snow in a storehouse. I am not smart enough for ALS, but God, who created all, knows all and controls all and is absolutely using His vast intelligence to work this situation together for His glory and our good. He is. Because He's brilliant. All creation—lands, seas, skies, and skeletal systems—has the fingerprints of God all over it.

God has infinite intelligence, and the more I learn about the vastness of His knowledge, the more certain I become of the smallness of mine. This is not a sad discovery but a happy one because it releases me from feeling responsible for running the universe while also struggling to understand my seventh grader's math homework.

Psalm 147 paints a portrait of the limitless knowledge and understanding of God. Scholars believe that it was written after Israel's Babylonian captivity, as a broken-but-breathing remnant of Hebrews emerged from the wreckage. The psalmist begins by declaring that God is determined to rebuild, gather, heal, and bind up the people and the nation. This is a beautiful promise of restoration. But then the psalmist explores the wonders of creation, exclaiming that God knows the stars, having named each and every one. The writer tells of His knowledge about everything, from clouds to cows to weather systems.

Why does the psalmist include these details about the enormity of God's work in creation when speaking to people still nursing their battle wounds? I suspect it's so they will understand that God, who is able and attentive to the hunger pangs of ravens, is more than capable of rebuilding their broken lives. The psalmist piles proof upon proof that God is smart enough for every situation we will ever face. We can lean hard on this assurance.

Read this verse out loud so that your ears can hear it and your heart can absorb it:

> God's love is meteoric,
>     his loyalty astronomic,
> His purpose titanic,
>     his verdicts oceanic.
> Yet in his largeness
>     nothing gets lost;
> Not a man, not a mouse,
>     slips through the cracks. (Psalm 36:5-6, MSG)

God's knowledge spans the vast expanse of the galaxy, but it also extends into the deepest reaches of our hearts. Not only does He see all these things but He is smart enough to care for them flawlessly. Be encouraged today, friend: The God Who Fights For You runs the small things as well as the big things. His knowledge is infinite yet intimate, and you have not escaped His notice, His care, or His kindness.

More reading: 1 Samuel 2:3; 2 Samuel 22:27; Job 26:3; Psalm 136:5-9; 147; Isaiah 55:8-9; Matthew 10:30; 1 John 3:19-20

## WORTH PONDERING

1. If you could ask God for the answer to a question that is beyond your intelligence, what would it be?

2. If God knows everything, then He already knows the battle you face and how it will end. How does this impact the way you face your fight?

## CHAPTER 26

*The God Who Fights For You . . .*

# TURNS BROKENNESS INTO BEAUTY

We all enjoy books and movies that let us ride along with a character from "down and out" to "top of the heap." We love to see the gears of power shift as fortunes change and, finally, the glass slipper fits and all is right with the world. Imagine Cinderella's story without the trouble and tragedy. A beautiful girl from a supportive family goes to a wonderful ball and falls in love with the handsome prince who immediately (yawn) falls in love with her. Take away the tension, and Cinderella becomes boring and maybe even a bit annoying. The conflict-free love story of a princess might be happy, but it will never be epic.

The more I read the Bible, the more convinced I am that God also loves a great story. God is a turning God. He turns death to life, ashes to beauty, and sin to celebration. In His very first recorded act, He turns a formless void into a universe teeming with life and order. He creates a world with sky and sea, sun and moon, and then fills it with color, sound, and movement. He seeds the skies with stars and not just a scattering but a septillion (that's a 1 with 24 zeroes) and then gives each one a name (see Psalm 147:4). He turns His craftsmanship to lions and lizards and butterflies. While the world could easily have gotten by with just one butterfly, He created 20,000 kinds of butterflies. He created ecosystems and respiratory systems and so much more than we would ever need because He turns empty into full. He is a turning God.

See for yourself:

My flesh and my heart may fail,
but God is the strength of my heart,
my portion forever. (Psalm 73:26, emphasis added)

You intended to harm me, but God intended it for good to accomplish what is now being done, the saving of many lives. (Genesis 50:20, NIV, emphasis added)

And my favorite:

They took Him down from the tree and put Him in a tomb. But God raised Him from the dead. (Acts 13:29-30, emphasis added)

On the victory side of these verses is the strength of God, the saving of many lives, and a resurrected Savior. In these things we rejoice, but prior to the rejoicing came discouragement, imprisonment, and three days in a dark tomb. Before the prodigal son feasted on the celebration lamb, he ate with the pigs. Before the beauty comes the ashes, and before the ashes? Fire.

The triumph is in the tension, and the road we walk on the way to the victory we long for is not wasted. Not for a minute.

> We rejoice in the hope of the glory of God. And not only that, but we also rejoice in our afflictions, because we know that affliction produces endurance, endurance produces proven character, and proven character produces hope. (Romans 5:2-4)

God uses the tension before the turning to work in us. To change us. To grow us. He is always active in our lives, winning every battle for His name's sake (which is the best "sake" ever). He is producing something outrageously beautiful:

> You were dead. . . . But God, who is rich in mercy, because of His great love that He had for us, made us alive with the Messiah. (Ephesians 2:1,4-5)

From the very beginning of time, He has planned to turn your story into an epic tale of great reversal. Maybe you should trust Him with the pen. He is writing a masterpiece.

More reading: the book of Esther; Isaiah 61:1-7

## WORTH PONDERING

1. What parts of your story would you like to go back and change?

2. Can you see ways God has turned bad for good in your life?

## CHAPTER 27

# *The God Who Fights For You...*
# DOES NOT CHANGE

*Immutability* is a big word. And it would be an insufferably boring word, except the validity of all the other words we've applied to God's character up until now hinge on this one. Simply put, *immutability* means that God will never change. The God Who Fights For You is who He is, always and forever, amen. Everything else we know of Him is set securely, permanently, and immovably in the cement of His immutability. Read this big truth: "I, Yahweh, have not changed" (Malachi 3:6).

The famous nineteenth-century preacher Charles Spurgeon said this in a sermon on God's immutability:

> He loves as much now as he did then, and when suns shall cease to shine, and moons to show their feeble light, he still shall love on for ever and for ever. Take any one attribute of God, and I will write *semper idem* on it (always the same). Take any one thing you can say of God now, and it may be said not only in the dark

past, but in the bright future it shall always remain the same: "I am Jehovah, I change not."[1]

I suspect that we undervalue the importance of God's unchanging nature, perhaps because it's a foreign concept to us. In our world, everything changes. The trees in our backyards are not the same trees they were last year. Concrete sidewalks erode beneath the weight of weather and walkers. Boulders fall from mountains. Stars burn out in the galaxy. And people— people are constantly changing. Our bodies bend and stoop; our emotions roll like the tides; our moods and relationships and hair colors change. I cannot think of a single thing, whether person or particle, that remains unchanged over time.

But God. His love, kindness, and character do not, will not, *cannot* budge. Can you fathom it? James, half brother of Jesus, says it in the most beautiful way:

Every generous act and every perfect gift is from above, coming down from the Father of lights; with Him there is no variation or shadow cast by turning. (James 1:17)

Do you hear the rock-solid certainty in these words? Not even a sliver of a shadow in God's perfection. This is huge truth if we'll grab on to it, because it means that once we understand who God is and how He works, that knowledge is ours to keep. Having an immovable awareness of His immutability will keep us from judging His character according to our circumstances on any given day. As He has always been, so He will always be. Count on it.

More reading: Numbers 23:19; 2 Timothy 2:13; Hebrews 13:5

## WORTH PONDERING

1. Has anyone ever had a change of heart concerning you? How did it impact you?

2. Sometimes we look at *unchanging* as synonymous with *uninteresting.* List some positive words that describe God's immutability.

3. Why is God's unchanging nature especially important during battle seasons?

## CHAPTER 28

*The God Who Fights For You . . .*
# HATES ONE THING

God makes no compromises with sin. Period.

This characteristic of His nature frequently gets misinterpreted and misused, so it often gets relegated it to the fine print of sermon notes. Because it's been wrongly used as a weapon against those with whom we disagree, the church frequently tries to smooth over God's stubborn refusal to compromise by aiming the spotlight exclusively on His more feel-good characteristics, such as grace and compassion. The problem, though, is that unless we take a good, hard look at this characteristic, we'll never comprehend how desperately we need the others. Consequently, the more we understand this one, the more overwhelmed and thankful we'll feel for the others.

So please remember what you already believe about the goodness, love, and protective nature of God as we look at the evidence that He is also uncompromising. He has a specific viewpoint on sin, and it has not and will not change, despite the events of our world or the evolution of our culture. It was the same before the fall of humankind as it was after the Cross and as it is today. (The Cross changed God's response to *us*, not His view of sin.) Read God's words to the children of Israel as they prepared to enter into the Promised Land:

> If your heart turns away and you do not listen and you are led astray to bow down to other gods and worship them, I tell you today that you will certainly perish and will not live long in the land you are entering to possess across the Jordan. I call heaven and earth as witnesses against you today that I have set before you life and death, blessing and curse. Choose life so that you and your descendants may live. (Deuteronomy 30:17-19)

Very clear instructions, yes? But when we fast-forward to Judges, just one book and one generation later, we discover that Israel had not obeyed the mandate. The Hebrews had adopted a new, polytheistic view of worship and abandoned the very Giver of the land they now possessed. Somewhere along the way, they'd become convinced that His blessing was not contingent on their behavior in any way. God's response to them shows us that, though they were willing to compromise their end of the bargain, He was not willing to compromise on His:

> Whenever the Israelites went out, the LORD was against them and brought disaster on them, just as He had promised and sworn to them. So they suffered greatly. (Judges 2:15)

God keeps His promise; He would not bless their sin. In 1 Samuel 15, King Saul compromised his level of obedience in a big way. Here is God's response through the prophet Samuel:

> The LORD has torn the kingship of Israel away from you today and has given it to your neighbor who is better than you. Furthermore, the Eternal One of Israel does not lie or change His mind, for He is not man who changes His mind. (verses 28-29)

From cover to cover, the Bible presents consistent and undeniable evidence that God *hates* sin. I believe He hates it because it hurts us, and that's why He refuses to compromise His response toward it. But, you might be thinking, *What about grace? Doesn't grace soften the blow?* No. It's grace, as poured out through the blood of Jesus on the cross, that *absorbs* the blow. "He made the One who did not know sin to be sin for us, so that we might become the righteousness of God in Him" (2 Corinthians 5:21). His death on the cross did not redefine sin or change God's viewpoint of it but rather opened a way of forgiveness *for* sin and freedom *from* its evil clutches.

An insidious deception creeps through much theology today, cheapening the grace of the Cross by suggesting that sin is no longer the problem it once was. Perhaps in response to fire-and-brimstone preaching that's short on love, we have recast the idea of God's grace as something that eliminates sin rather than what it really is: the thing that activates forgiveness. Grace positions us within reach of God's mercy; it does not remove our desperate need for it. If we overlook the evidence of

God's uncompromising view of sin, we will leave the gift of grace unopened and undervalued. On the flip side, when we're willing to see our sin the way God sees it, we can begin to understand the depths of eternal meaning found in the words of Paul:

> When the kindness of God our Savior and His love
> for mankind appeared,
> He saved us —
> not by works of righteousness that we had done,
> but according to His mercy
> through the washing of regeneration
> and renewal by the Holy Spirit.
> He poured out this Spirit on us abundantly
> through Jesus Christ our Savior,
> so that having been justified by His grace,
> we may become heirs with the hope of eternal life. (Titus 3:4-7)

When we distort God's view of sin, we disconnect from the miraculous power of redemption. I am challenged by these words of Dietrich Bonhoeffer, which occupy a prominent place above my desk and remind me every day that I am bought with the price paid by an uncompromising God:

> Grace is costly because it calls us to follow, and it is grace
> because it calls us to follow Jesus Christ. It is costly because it
> costs a man his life, and it is grace because it gives a man the
> only true life. It is costly because it condemns sin and grace

because it justifies the sinner. Above all, it is costly because it cost God the life of his Son: "ye were bought at a price," and what has cost God much cannot be cheap for us. Above all, it is grace because God did not reckon his Son too dear a price to pay for our life, but delivered him up for us. Costly grace is the Incarnation of God.[1]

The more I get to know the character of God, the more I realize how the gift of grace makes our relationship with Him scandalously lopsided. He brings forgiveness, redemption, and healing, and all He asks from me is the admission that I can't save myself. To be known and loved by the uncompromising God is a prize worth more than gold.

More reading: Numbers 23:19; Psalm 15:9; Matthew 7:13-14; Hebrews 1:9; 7:21

## WORTH PONDERING

1. How do you think our world has redefined sin? How has this view of sin impacted the way people value grace?

2. Can you see any places in your life or thoughts where you have allowed compromise?

3. Have you ever faced a battle that was the result of a compromised belief? What were the results?

## CHAPTER 29

# *The God Who Fights For You . . .*
# WANTS YOU TO WIN

The essence of our existence—all that we think, dream, feel, and breathe—is rooted in God. Read this verse out loud slowly and intentionally, letting the weight of the words take shape in your thinking:

> What was from the beginning,
> what we have heard,
> what we have seen with our eyes,
> what we have observed
> and have touched with our hands,
> concerning the Word of life —
> that life was revealed,
> and we have seen it
> and we testify and declare to you
> the eternal life that was with the Father
> and was revealed to us. (1 John 1:1-2)

Now read these simple but significant words from Job:

> The life of every living thing is in His hand, as well as the breath
> of all mankind. (Job 12:10)

All life and all breath—yours, mine, and every other creature's—is in God's hands. He is life and He gives life. We are His creation and His prize, and it's tragic that people so often pit Him against humanity as if He is always frowning at our freedom, fun, and happiness. God is positively pro-human, which is why He is anti-sin. His goal for us is exceedingly abundant life (see John 10:10), and He is against anything that prevents human flourishing.

*Flourishing* is a grand word that means "to be in a vigorous state; thrive; to be in one's prime; to grow luxuriantly or thrive in growth as a plant."[1] Sounds fantastic, right? It's exactly how I want my life to look, but when rightly considered, I believe that *flourishing* is different from *happiness*, which means "delighted, pleased, or glad." Though I want to live in a way that leads to thriving, I often choose whatever will make me immediately happy instead. Moses is listed as a hero of faith because he chose a life of flourishing obedience instead of temporary pleasure:

> By faith Moses . . . chose to suffer with the people of God rather
> than to enjoy the short-lived pleasure of sin. For he considered
> the reproach because of the Messiah to be greater wealth than
> the treasures of Egypt, since his attention was on the reward.
> (Hebrews 11:24-26)

Read the last six words again. Moses made a decision to focus on the supernatural prize offered by his life-loving God. He was not dead to the allure of sin, but he knew that God had called him to something bigger than happiness. In fact, God had a much bigger win in mind. Moses' decision to partner with God's plan for his life led to freedom for an entire nation and the eventual possession of the Promised Land.

The God Who Fights For You *is* life and is therefore *for* life. He is for thriving. He wants you to win every battle, but He knows that you can't do it on your own. None of us can. We need the Author of Life to show us the way to a flourishing life. We desperately need His wisdom and power at work in the everyday walking-talking-working-sleeping business of living.

God is qualified to give abundant life; we are not because our humanity will always drive us toward choices that create temporary pleasure and short-circuit eternal treasure:

> As for you, you were dead in your transgressions and sins, in which you used to live when you followed the ways of this world and of the ruler of the kingdom of the air. . . . But because of his great love for us, God, who is rich in mercy, made us alive with Christ. (Ephesians 2:1-2,4-5, NIV)

Read that verse again. The first line gets me every time: "as for you, *you were dead.*" The bottom line to all that we've read and studied thus far is this: We were dead, but God is life. Real life both now and in eternity is sourced in the Son of God and His work on the cross. Only the God who created life could orchestrate so beautiful a plan. Only He could pen so great a redemption story. He came for the living dead to make us fully alive and flourishing, now and forever. Amen.

More reading: Psalm 12:17; 56:13; 103:4; John 1:4; 3:36; 10:10; 1 John 5:20

## WORTH PONDERING

1. On a scale of 1 to 10, how flourishing is your life?

2. How connected do you feel to God's desire that you flourish and grow?

3. How might you lean in more fully to His desires for your life this week?

## CHAPTER 30

*The God Who Fights For You . . .*

# NEVER FORGETS
# YOU (EVER)

It was a beautiful night and a beautiful event, crafted by beautiful people. It was also unspeakably sad. Our dear friends had gathered fifty or sixty people to their home on a Saturday night for a bon voyage party. They weren't going on an extended vacation or moving out of state; they were going to prison. None of us knew how long they would be there, but we knew it wouldn't be a short stay.

A four-year court case over their involvement in a failed real estate development had produced many things in their lives. They had grown closer to one another and closer to their dearest friends, and they had been drawn to a real and intimate relationship with Jesus in a way they had never before known. They lost much: millions of dollars, their reputation, and their freedom. They also found much: salvation. I feel certain they would want me to tell you that the finding was worth the losing.

The evening was uncharacteristically warm and sunny for April in our Oregon mountain town. As Steve and I drove to the party, too sad for conversation, I remember thinking that God must have intervened in the weather, knowing that none of us would have made it through that night if the sky was crying too. Cars lined the driveway and overflowed onto both sides of the street. People crowded into all the corners of their house and spilled out onto the deck. Our friends floated through this sea of people so dear to their hearts, hugging, crying, and saying tender words. Then, as the sun was sinking low and spreading red and orange flames across the sky, the whole sobbing lot of us circled around our friends and witnessed the renewal of their vows to one another, promising to love, honor, cherish, and remember. Though they knew that a long separation was coming, they vowed to remember their devotion every single day, and they sealed those vows with kisses and tears. It was one of the most meaningful moments I've ever witnessed.

The next day, Steve and I met them for coffee before they drove three hours to the city, where judgment awaited them. They were to be taken into custody immediately upon sentencing, so I knew this was my last chance to see them for many years. Steve, however, is counting his days carefully, and this changed the moment dramatically. There, in a small Starbucks, we gathered our chairs in a tight circle and my husband spoke his truest heart. "I am so proud of you," he said as tears rolled down our faces unchecked. "You have grown so close to Jesus during your suffering. You have let Him use this in your life to make you more like Him. And I know that this is so hard, but it has a beginning, middle, and end. You will grow strong and He will be with you, and I hope that I will be able to hug you when you get out." He took a deep breath as we all held ours. "But if that doesn't happen, know that I am in the cloud of witnesses and am cheering you on. I will not forget you. Jesus will not forget you. You are loved."

I cried myself to sleep that night, thinking of my friends, my beloved, life, and its fleeting, fickle friendships. I prayed until I could think of nothing more to ask of God on behalf of these people I loved. The next day, they were sentenced to many years in a minimum-security federal prison. They each received much longer sentences than any of us had anticipated. The friends who attended the party are working hard to not only remember them but also remind them we remember them. We send letters and books and prayers into the prison cells we cannot enter and they cannot exit. I've asked the Lord many times to bring them to the front of my mind—to not let me get busy with life and forget about them. I think this is a good prayer because it's essentially asking to be like Him. He does not forget us. It is part of His character to remember. Look at these beautiful words to a disobedient, rebellious, and in-captivity Israel:

> Zion said, "I don't get it. God has left me.
> > My Master has forgotten I even exist."
>
> "Can a mother forget the infant at her breast,
> > walk away from the baby she bore?
> But even if mothers forget,

I'd never forget you — never.

Look, I've written your names on the backs of my hands."

(Isaiah 49:14-16, MSG)

Can you imagine a couple in the hospital, packing up their flowers and balloons, their suitcase, and hospital paperwork, their slippers and wallet, but forgetting to take their precious new baby? Never. We humans may forget to pick up milk at the grocery store or pay a parking ticket. We may even forget some dear things such as our friends who have been gone for a long time. Our minds grow fuzzy and full, and we forget what we should remember and remember what we should forget. I do it all the time, but God does not. We are to Him like a newborn baby, completely dependent on His attention and affection, and He could never forget us. Our names are engraved on His hand. He always remembers.

He will never forget you — not in good times or bad, in war or in peace, in deepest joy or darkest night. You might close the cover of this book and forget all you read about God, but God, who knows every page of your story, will never forget you. If you possess that one truth, you are already ahead in battle because you'll never have to fight alone. His thoughts toward you are certain and outnumber the sand on the shore (see Psalm 139:17-18) and He will never, ever forget you. That's who He is and who He will always be. You can count on it.

More reading: Leviticus 26:44-45; 1 Samuel 1:19; Psalm 103:13-14; 111:5

## WORTH PONDERING

1. Have you ever felt forgotten by God? What made you feel this way? When you read Isaiah 49:14-16, do you feel that it applies to you? Why or why not?

# CONCLUSION

Here, at the end of our journey together, I want to tell you about the constant prayer that has been my companion throughout the process of writing this book. I have not prayed that you would find all the answers about God or that you would be convinced about any one detail of His character in particular. I have not prayed that you would establish a rock-solid theology or an unshakable faith in His goodness. My one big Ask from God has been that these words would stir up a passion for the pursuit—that you would discover angles and aspects of His character that create a desire to know more.

My greatest joy would be that the end of this book marks the beginning of a long, happy search for more truth, more beauty, and a deeper friendship with Jesus than ever before. I wish for you a divine discontent that keeps you seeking, finding, and sharing your discoveries of His goodness. And I pray that every nugget of knowledge you gain of our Great Commander would cause you to face every fight with faith.

My family and I remain on the battlefield. Our story has no resolution yet, but it does have a happy ending because we are confident in the One who is holding the pen. We have many questions about evil, sickness, suffering, and sorrow in our world, but our theology has grown simpler and stronger every day of our fight. It is this: The God we serve is always and only good, and all He does is beautiful. Because of this we can say with certainty that the last line will read, "Happily ever after."

I'm praying that you know it too.

# NOTES

Chapter 3: Isn't Mad at You

1. James Strong, *Strong's Exhaustive Concordance of the Bible* (Nashville: Thomas Nelson, 1890), 108.
2. Frederick Dale Bruner, *The Gospel of John: A Commentary* (Grand Rapids, MI: Eerdmans, 2013), 509.
3. For more on God's view of sin, see Romans 28–29.

Chapter 12: Keeps Good Books

1. Learn more about Kings Kids Village at kingskidsvillage.org.
2. R. C. Sproul, *The Character of God* (Ann Arbor, MI: Servant, 1995), 103.
3. James Strong, *Strong's Exhaustive Concordance of the Bible* (Grand Rapids, MI: Baker, 1977), 23.
4. Strong, 43.

Chapter 13: Makes You Mighty

1. James Strong, *Strong's Exhaustive Concordance of the Bible* (Grand Rapids, MI: Baker, 1977), 16.
2. Strong, 24.

Chapter 18: Gives Good Directions
  1. James Strong, *Strong's Exhaustive Concordance of the Bible* (Grand Rapids, MI: Baker, 1977), 60.

Chapter 22: Defeats Darkness
  1. Frederick Dale Bruner, *The Christbook: Matthew 1-12* (Grand Rapids, MI: Eerdmans, 1987), 138.

Chapter 23: Gives You Rest
  1. Camille Peri, *10 Things to Hate About Sleep Loss*, www.webmd.com, 2010 (http://www.webmd.com/sleep-disor ders/excessive-sleepiness-10/10-results-sleep-loss?page=1).

Chapter 24: Can Be Trusted Completely
  1. Edward McKendree Bounds, *The Necessity of Prayer* (Grand Rapids, MI: Baker, 1976), 7.

Chapter 27: Does Not Change
  1. Rev. C. H. Spurgeon, New Park Street Chapel, Southwark, London, January 7, 1855, www.spurgeon.org/sermons.

Chapter 28: Hates One Thing
  1. Dietrich Bonhoeffer, *The Cost of Discipleship* (New York: Touchstone, 1959), 44–45.

Chapter 29: Wants You to Win
  1. *Webster's New College Dictionary*, Third Edition (Houghton, Harcourt, Mifflin, 2008), 439.

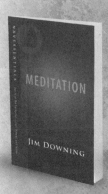